Journeys Beyond

Short stories and poems

To Rog and Diane,

Love,

Harvey

3rd Sept. 2016

Earlyworks Press

Copyright information

paperback ISBN 978-1-910841-37-2
first published August 2016
ebook available in various formats

Printed in the UK by
Catford Print

Published by Earlyworks Press
Creative Media Centre,
45 Robertson St, Hastings,
Sussex TN34 1HL

www.earlyworkspress.co.uk

Contents

The Teacher

by Jonathan Page

The teacher's back is like an upturned boat because he is walking in snow and must study the ground. Silver birches stand naked on the shore of the lake.

Two children watch the circle of their breath grow and diminish on the pane. It is almost more interesting than the mythic teacher, this huddling in puffa jackets over the iron lung of the radiator. The pin-prick cold that lives in the glass. What is the old man doing? What he always does at three, when he thinks all the children have gone – he is going to the lake.

The boy turns to the girl, he thinks he leads. He is the energy that Emma who favours corners and books follows and animates. He is the actor, the velvet tan of his skin, the yellow wing of hair he sweeps from his eyes. She is the outside, where the light lies warm and quiet on the carpet in the school's library. She is more comfortable in empty rooms like this, where the day hangs shining in the windows and the laminate floor creaks like it felt them there. They are intimate and strange to each other, unlikely, natural. Jens says let's follow him and Emma says no no the taxi though it is already decided, the words are ritual. The taxi will have to wait.

The snow squeaks polystyrene under the teacher's feet. Fragments of snow have broken from the low ridges to either side of the path and lie in their perfect shadows. From the black hut of the school room he is knit with the ground, his progress uncanny. His breath smokes into existence against the birches. The same thoughts come to him at the same places and are less than thoughts or more than thoughts because of it, like prayer, or breath, half united with the world. The startling gravel of the shore and the firs that cover the hills on the farther side.

The boy and the girl stand afraid of their visibility in the snow. Jens wishes his coat was not red and Emma that hers was not black but what colour should they be. The teacher is kind but there is something desolate in him that the children find numinous. They quake with whispers, wriggles, chair-scrapes when they find him staring out at nothing in the middle of quiet reading. They fear the long dark in him then and so mock it. They lock unmerciful into their own space until he barks and they are themselves again. But he forgets. He forgets that this is what happens and their need to call out to him in rebellion. He often stands at the window, older than a teacher has rights to be.

Jens and Emma crunch into the path, scared at first, as if the path were his tail and he could feel their boots. The teacher is a mark under the lid of lake water, turning into the birch wood. Hurry Emma, come on. Though they move at the same speed it is what Jens in his role feels compelled to say and Emma expects to hear. They jog on the shining footsteps of the teacher, crushing the delicate walls. Emma thinks of an excuse to give him if he stops and turns and sees them. They have missed the taxi, they do not have a phone. She sees herself telling him this excuse, the old distant man with the lake at his back, she rehearses what she will say over and over and the excuse becomes half-real. The land shakes along with their breathing. Stop Emma. Stop. The boy's hand dramatic across the front of her coat. The teacher is inside the bars of the trees staring at the lake. What is he doing?

Their previous teacher disappeared, in the weeks before summer break. She dressed neatly and they listened to her long slim hands on the piano in the hall. She crouched by their tables and listened to them with her black eyes. She taught them for less than a year but the world looked like her, by the end. They came into class one day to find the head teacher's set smile: Miss Oster was sorry, she would miss them all, but she was poorly and could not teach them anymore. The head teacher's face was a dam that said there was another adult truth they could not ask for. When she turned to the window the lenses in her glasses turned white.

The old teacher is a moving slice of dark in the white trees. He is animal like a bear or deer. The ground is whitened by winter but there is little snow in here. The children's boots shuffle small drifts of crisp brown leaves and they are afraid of the ricochet crack of sticks. A cracked stick is his voice, seeing them, but he does not see them. Over the rise and fall, the stones standing clean and watchful among the trees, they see the lake again. It is an opaque grey blue, thicker than summer water and more distant. It is paired with the sky and the ghosts of the mountains at the base of the sky. Emma wants to go back, a story is all very well but this is not the story. It is Jens that keeps them going, he is always in the next dip and she cannot catch him to tell him to stop. The need and the trying are repeated over and over up to the shore. The water comes in small bites over the shining gravel and the roots of trees are exposed red hair. Jens is still and staring and she forgets to tell him they must stop. He is like a deer now. What is faked is also numinous. What is faked can turn real, that is the power of games. Look he whispers there he is.

The teacher is sitting at a picnic table. The swimming jetty marches over its black self into the solid water of the lake and the water smacks and peels from its pillars. Emma notices the dead flowers tied to the leg of the table, their drained reds and the live pink ribbon. What is he doing? Jens says it for the shared heat of their faces and to oppose the interruptions of the lake. The way it throws flats of water onto the sand. He says it because they are in the story the class has made up about the teacher: there is a body in the woods or else treasure he must check on and that is why he goes there. The story is only real in the heat of its telling, it dies when the children are alone. But the class knows something, the explanation warps about the hidden and the feared, and the story burns into truth.

The teacher watches the stones of his fists on the table. It is too cold to be gloveless but the ache removes him from himself and carries him into the long empty sight of water. They swam here in the summer, after she had persuaded him to apply for her old post. She gave no sign, she was happier, at surface. He thinks of her in her red costume, the goose-bumps on her thin arms as she hauled herself up, shivering, onto the jetty. The way they huddled close to the disposable barbecue for warmth as the sun bled into the lake. There was no sign or none he wanted to see.

Jens and Emma have no plan for what comes next. Snow is falling in the lake but not on them, it covers the water with black granules. They want to look into the cold that is filling them as much as they are supposed to look at the teacher. That is when he sees them. They have grown lazy about their invisibility, they wriggle in the heat of their jackets against the winter in their knees, and then they see that he sees. The weight of his stillness is what tells them.

Jens, what are you doing?

Emma's hand is shed violently from his coat and he is running towards the table. If he sees them he is guilty, it converts his shame. The bare earth he saw in the woods is converted in his mind to potential graves. Every stone hides a faceless child or Miss Oster. The teacher stands amazed as the boy roars out of the mute day and hurls his whole body at the table. He watches speechless as the boy wrestles with the pockets of his jacket, a growling animal, and brings out a pen knife. It takes forever to fold out the blade.

Jens what are you doing here? And Emma. You should be at home, your parents…

You killed her! You killed her and put her in the woods!

Emma hears the story die on the body of the teacher, as she knew it would die, but she is not yet out of its glamour. The teacher is too much a part of the snow that comes vanishing down about their shoulders. The ancient threat of the wood and the cold water is presented to her in him.

Give me the knife Jens. What do you think you are doing?

You killed Miss Oster. She went and then you came and you go into the woods every day.

Jens starts to cry, breaks open and red in the open with his hands limp at his side. All the anger and sense is gone in the sentence. The teacher picks at the dead flowers unconsciously, which shudder and will not be taken. Emma comes up to Jens but he is untouchable, and when she looks at the teacher for direction the teacher sees it all.

So, you are detectives. You stayed behind to follow me. I didn't think anybody knew about my walks.

Where is Miss Oster?

Where is she Emma? Yes. All right. Miss Oster. Sofie Oster.

The children sit opposite him at the table and for a while it does not seem necessary to say anything. It is possible that they will all get up and walk silently back to the school, because the teacher is their teacher again and they are children. But they sit too long at the table for that to be possible. The teacher speaks softly at his reddening hands. Miss Oster was poorly, not in the body, you know, but inside, in her soul. She was the saddest a person can be, she was sad for years, and nothing seemed to help her, you understand? Because he does not, he circles the place and cannot name it. This is his story and that is the truth he can show them. He tells them that he was once Miss Oster's boyfriend and that afterwards he was still her friend. The children stare at him, looking for the stranger that has entered the old man. He was her boyfriend? Yes. A long time ago. We taught together at another school, years before you were born. Was Miss Oster old then? This second mystery has almost replaced the first. It is a friendly mystery, the one curated by their parents, their older siblings. Emma, forgetting where they are, smiles broadly. But the teacher goes on: she died, this summer. She asked me to apply for her post here and I did, I did it for her. I did not see it then but I think she was making sure things were tidy before she went away. She was always very tidy, much tidier than me. She loved her class and wanted them looked after.

How did she die?

Jens remembers he is accusing his teacher of a crime. His fists mirror those of the teacher's on the table. It is no good treating him like a boy so he talks to him like a man. She was a good swimmer, we swam all the time this summer. Late, when the families had gone home. It was like any other evening. She seemed happy. I thought something good had happened but it was only that she had decided. She waited until I had gone home and then she.

He cannot say anything else. He wrenches at the flowers until the top half tears from the ribbon and then lays them on the table. Emma says: she drowned then, in the lake, and now you are sad. Yes I am sad Emma. You are not going to kill yourself are you? Her hand tops his, he did not realise he was scratching at the wood of the table. No of course not. I am sad but I am not sad like Miss Oster, like Sofie. Good. Because you must not be that sad.

Her look is fierce and so is the boy's and he smiles at their appropriation of him.

Now we must go home. Your parents will be worried.

They walk back through the woods to the shining plain of snow in front of the school. Jens pushes his gloves on the teacher and the old teacher wears them for a few minutes – they do not pull down over the width of his hands – to prove he is in good faith.

Roxanne Riding Hood

by Bruce Harris

Things went on very late at the Club that night, I remember. Nothing particularly unusual about that; more than once, I've staggered back to my dressing room and fallen asleep on the couch I was benevolently allowed – eventually. Nice enough man, Dave Sorrell, if fat and overly inclined to cigars; he will come in at times whiffing like an ashtray.

'What's it for, Rox?' he says suspiciously.

'Listen, David, it's a little couch about five feet long and a foot wide. I'm a drag act, not a contortionist. Rest, David, that's what it's for. And somewhere for my visiting admirers to sit, of course. They come to pay their respects to one of London's leading drag artistes and they're stood there holding bouquets like spare pricks at the fair. It's just not polite.'

So I got my couch, and sometimes, by the time I've had a shower and changed sex, I just drop off until daylight and wander home past the coughing winos, the maniacal joggers and the bleary-eyed dog walkers. Or I drop off during the de-dragging process and wake up with one stocking on and one stocking off and mascara running down my face like the Bride of Frankenstein.

I needed to get home not too late on this night though, because I was due a visit from my brother Tom, who's one of the good guys. He's married now, to a sort of Gorgon called Ellen who gives me her death stare whenever she sees me in drag, mainly because I look better in women's clothes than she does. She's got small boobs and big feet; whatever she puts on, she looks like a duck with an identity crisis. What Tom sees in her I don't know, but there you go. You can love your relatives to bits, but you can't edit their taste in people.

Tom's an easy-going guy, a few years younger than me. Thirty's a recent trauma for him and a fading horizon for me. I'll have to move on from femmes fatales to distinguished ladies soon enough, I dare say, but the long legs are still up to the mark. *A Monroe voice and the legs to match*, said the *Evening Revue*, not that long ago. *Roxanne aka Paul Stanmore must put in some gym hours*. Well, yes, I suppose gymnastics is one word for it.

X years ago, when I was fifteen and he was thirteen, Tom walked in on me trying on two of Mum's dresses. I normally took precautions, but

Mum had picked up this slinky backless thing which I just had to see myself in, and I didn't hear him come in.

'You big puff,' he said, but not in a hostile way. "Live and let live" has always been Tom. He kept my secret for as long as I needed him to, bless him. He would even tell me what my bum looked big in, if perhaps not in quite those words.

Anyway, the Gorgon sometimes goes off to get her snakes checked out or something, and we brothers do the town for a day or two, catching up with each other's lives. He works in TV now, some digital lot, and it can all be quite fascinating.

So, this night, I woke myself up with a cold shower – I've done that from school onwards, when it was a reliable way of not getting a bonk on after PE with naked boys in every direction. I went towards the stage door, a shorter way than the front entrance, and I could hear some kind of trouble going on. Life around the Club can get a bit lively at the weekend, with kids off their face on booze and whatever else is their fancy.

Stage door to main street is seventy or so yards of wide alley which normally takes me about twenty seconds, once I've got the sensible shoes back on. I'd only gone half way along this night when two youths, both about nineteen, by the look of them, suddenly appeared in front and beside me.

'I've seen his picture without his slap on. God, it's Poxy Roxy, the drag act.'

He seemed to be addressing his mate as God, though settling for a deity with bad breath and jeans that look like they've been shat in seems to me to sell yourself short. God then says, 'how would you like us to kick the shit out of you, Roxy, you sad old queer?'

I took the question to be rhetorical, because action followed immediately, his mate with an arm around my neck, him fixing to punch me in the guts.

Maybe they were just being playful, and since I knew the police hovered around the Club on weekend nights, I wasn't too bothered, and I was even less so when a policeman appeared at the end of the alley. All the same, they were being very rude and unpleasant. Boys being boys is all very well, but I've had this stuff since schooldays and know something about taking care of myself. I've also taken self-defence classes with a gym instructor called Kevin. Both the classes and Kevin turned out to be worthwhile investments.

'We need to achieve mastery of a series of difficult positions,' said Kevin, and I thought how absolutely I agreed with him. Once on to the more advanced stuff, self-defence that is, it included what he called 'simultaneous counter movements', one of which was a quick succession of elbow and fist. The boy behind me was still trying to lock his arms around me, bless him, but I am always aware of any male genitalia in my vicinity, and swinging my right elbow into his with some oompty behind it made him temporarily lose interest in the proceedings. Elbow immediately followed by fist, as my left one swung round and connected right between God's eyes. He sort of went cross-eyed, exhaled a rancid, beer-sodden gasp and fell to his knees, presenting an irresistible opportunity to bring my other fist into play by banging it straight into his earhole.

By the time the policeman decided to make a token effort and started sauntering towards us, Boy One was being sick, one hand on his throat and the other between his legs – another quite neat simultaneous counter movement, I thought, and God was having a snooze on his back and gurgling now and then.

Someone shouted 'George?' and a second policeman appeared, though in plain clothes; I could tell he was a policeman because he knew the first policeman's name was George. You don't go round shouting "George" at policemen on the off chance that their names might be George. They both stood looking at me, and I was debating whether or not to do a little tap dance, when the uniformed one spoke.

'These two toe-rags were setting about this gentleman, it seemed, sir. I was about to offer assistance when it became plain that assistance wasn't required.'

'You obviously know how to take care of yourself, sir,' said plain clothes. Relaxed, even voice. Very un-rozzer like. 'Do you want to press charges?'

'No, I don't think so, officer. Lot of time and fuss. Just tell the breath monster when he wakes up that I recommend Listerine. And a new pair of jeans.'

And off I wandered, to be bright-eyed and bushy-tailed for our Tom in the morning, thinking no more of it until Dave the boss came into my dressing room a few nights later, bringing with him that subtle ashtray aroma.

'There's a policeman here wanting to see you, Rox,' he says. 'What have you been up to, you naughty girl?'

I was stripped down to my knickers and socks, and I was just about to throw a wobbly about knocking on bloody doors before coming through them when a quiet voice sounded off-stage, just outside the door.

'Mr Stanmore isn't in any trouble. I'm here to ask for his help.'

That unhurried, laid back voice again, which still carried authority, like he knew what he was talking about without having to shout it out. I knew immediately that I'd heard it before, and curiosity overcame indignation.

'OK, Dave, send him in, that's if he can cope with an artiste in his knickers.'

I was removing a difficult eyelash when he appeared in the mirror behind me, and I recognised the shape of him, which is most of what I saw that night. The full on facial revealed a thirty-something guy, clean shaven, with calm brown eyes and an intelligent, thoughtful face. For a policeman. Nuff said. I've had dealings with a few in my time, and not always harmoniously. He was slim built, one of these bantam weight guys who can run all day and do something else all night, if you know what I mean.

'Detective Inspector Sam Warren,' he said. 'Are you OK after the other night, or were there any afters, aches and pains, what have you?'

I turned and we shook hands. My instinct was to like him, but I've been around a while, and I always reserve judgement.

'No, I was alright. My brother was visiting, which is always a morale booster. If you can squeeze a place on that couch among all my debris, sit down, Inspector.'

'Sam,' he said, and if that didn't impress me enough, he shot such an unfeigned, natural smile at me as he sat that I could feel a heartstring or two tweaking away. I had to remind myself that this guy was a policeman. He reached into his coat pocket.

'I made them write this to you, when they'd sobered up in the morning. One of them was quite a soft spoken, decent lad with an apprenticeship and desperate not to lose it. One of these kids who just shouldn't drink because they can't take it. He went out on someone's stag night, lost the rest of them and then met up with the one you called a breath monster, a kid not long out of a Young Offenders' Institution. The place did what they do sometimes, and sent him out in a bigger mess than when he went in. The apprentice did the letter; the other one just signed it.'

I read the letter, written in a sort of semi-kiddie scrawl, with mistakes like "appology", "stag nite", "stupidness". Undertaking to do "anything" to make it up. One or two ideas occurred, but I've never been much of a twink fancier, personally, and then there'd be that halitosis. I remembered some dreadful old joke about the asthmatic rent boy who came in short pants, and I felt a bit queasy for a minute. Then the absurdity and pathos of it got to me, these two nearly-kids rampaging around, out of their minds on booze and pretending to be thugs, and the silly boys succeeded in touching me more effectively than they did on the night. I came over all moist-eyed and silly for a minute. My new mate Sam the policeman didn't do what most men do in the company of tears, look at their shoes and pretend it's not happening; he just watched me patiently and uncritically until the weepy moment had passed.

'You said you wanted to ask me something, Inspect – er – Sam,' I said.

'Yes,' he said. 'But sit down for a moment; are you sure you're OK?'

This was my kind of policeman. I swivelled my chair round to face him.

'Yes, I'm fine. Being a soppy cow occasionally helps me get into the part. What did you want to ask me?'

'You probably know that some of the street girls round here have been attacked recently. It's happening now almost every week.'

'Yes, I know,' I said, and I did. 'Some of the girls get in here. They're very concerned, to put it mildly. One or two have decided to stop trading for a while, though I know for a fact that they'll struggle without it.'

'Well, I'm determined that I am going to catch this guy,' Sam said, leaning forward, and the glint in his eyes spoke of something rather personal. 'He's a bastard, and a cunning bastard with it. So far, he's stopped short of rape, though not by much; his attacks are both physical and sexual assaults and he might well rape yet. He suddenly appears behind the girls without them having seen him, which suggests to us some connection with one of the buildings around here. We've never yet seen an escape car or a pursuit from the scene of the crime. Some of the girls think he gets off mostly on their fear of him, their willingness to oblige to avoid further violence. A demented sort of mastery, I suppose.'

'So how can I help? I'd like to help; those girls are my friends.'

'We've given the girls alarm buttons which connect to us and we're running a car through the areas, mainly Darrington Street round the back of this Club, to tell you the truth, at least three times a night. I haven't got the resources to just leave a car here every night. But every time it happens, the whole thing's over by the time we get to the girls, and he's disappeared again. We've got descriptions, and by now we know pretty well how he dresses and what he looks like. We've checked on local work places, but a lot of them are pubs and clubs and we can't trace their entire weekend clientele. I need someone who can batter him about enough, or at least hold him up enough, to give us time to get to him. He won't go anywhere near a man. But a man who can credibly look like a woman, and handle himself. That could be different.'

He looked me up and down, practically naked me, and that sent little currents of electric right through me. Not all guys who like dressing up as women are gay, that's true enough, but this one is, and interest is interesting. I'm currently not spoken for; I rarely am. I've never really got the hang of monogamy; millions of guys out there, and just one of them for the rest of my life? It's like a thirsty man allowing himself three drops a day. I just can't do it.

But, of course, for Sam this was about physique, not sex. Ho-hum.

'You're a fit guy, Mr Stanmore –'

'Paul.'

'You're a fit guy, Paul; a fit, well-built guy with no flab. For what we have in mind, it's you or a female police officer. At the moment, I've got two women in my team; one's in her forties and the other's in the early stages of pregnancy. I need a public-spirited citizen like yourself, as capable of laying out two guys in a few minutes as he is of looking like a beautiful woman, to aid the force. I need someone who can hold the guy up long enough for us to get to him. How about it?'

I looked at my face in the mirror. I'm a good-looking guy; I have to be for the feminine thing to happen. Having my face rearranged would put the whole act on hold; having my face seriously rearranged would finish it. Two kids so far gone they can hardly throw a punch, is one thing; a clever, ruthless guy, sober or on something – that's another.

Sam looked at me looking at myself, and for once misread the clues.

'OK,' he said. 'Thanks for hearing me out. I can understand you've got a living to make, like we all have.'

'No.' I faced him again. 'I just needed a moment. Like I said, those girls are my friends, and as you don't sound in the business of making judgments, I'll tell you that I used to do a little sex work myself. That's part of how I got to know how to protect what I need to protect. And I did come across the occasional type who wasn't just about a bit of SM, but got off on random violence. I generally don't mind what people get off on, but getting off on hurting and terrifying people isn't right. I'll do it, Sam. I'll talk to the girls, pick up a few tips and tell them to pass the word round so no-one thinks I'm some newbie trying to muscle in on them.'

Sam the policeman's hand on my bare shoulder; volts passing through me again. The last policeman's hand wasn't so friendly. I thought of asking what reward he had in mind, coming over all camp and suggestive. He might be amused, but that's all he'd be. So be it. I stopped thinking I could make the world the way I wanted it round about the age of eight.

We worked on it for the next three weeks. I talked to three of the girls who'd been attacked; same thing in every case. He'd suddenly come at them from behind, with his clenched fists and opened palms in combination; fusillades of random, indiscriminate blows, enough to be seriously distressing and cause injury. One of the girls – let's call her Jo – a tough Scouse lass, did attempt to fight back and ultimately fought him off, but she was bruised and out of action for a while. She said the answering back seemed to intensify his anger, but she at least wasn't sexually assaulted – humiliating, painful assaults, not enough for permanent damage, maybe, but as bad as it can get short of out and out rape. The girls said that the guy got off, visibly so, when he knew he had them in his power and they were submissive to him.

'His kicks are about being in charge,' said young Adele, probably no more than eighteen. 'The stupid thing is if it was just the kind of fiddling about he goes in for that he wanted to do, he could get it by paying for it; it's the taking it by force which is what it's about.'

'No, he's not a customer I've ever had,' said Jo. 'The other girls say the same. You remember something about each of them, usually the smell; the ones who smell bad, you don't do at all, but you remember the others all the same. Some of them are repeat trade, too, so you get to recognise things about them.'

We sweated away at it, with everyone sworn to secrecy. I haven't worked so hard since I last updated the act. I worked with the girls at a safe house the police had, and Dave Sorrell, who of course had been listening to my first conversation with Sam, was told to button it or have people looking into his – let's say flexible – interpretations of the licensing laws. And the dealers in his clubs, come to that.

The girls dressed me in street fashion, mostly clothes practical enough to prevent freezing to death, while still being enticing for the punters, which is not an easy combination. We worked on walking – the megaqueen way the drag artiste parades is not the way a working girl strides the streets; there are a lot of differences, some obvious, some subtle. I confessed that I already knew something about working the streets, and of course they all knew a few rent boys, so we kind of bonded into the sex workers' union.

Eventually, I was on for doing my patrol up and down Darrington Street, not so many yards away from the Club where I did my act, though I was pretty much unrecognisable from it. I went out for three nights, spread over a week, and I had to tell several generally very polite guys looking for "trade" that things weren't quite what they seemed; one started getting mouthy, but he moved on when I signalled towards the police car passing on its check up.

It wasn't looking as though the thing would happen, and I thought he would almost certainly have smelt a rat by now if he'd been watching what was going on. From the start, Sam and I had had the kind of relationship which allowed both of us to speak our minds, and I told him I thought the moment had gone; for all our efforts to keep the "project", as he called it, quiet, I felt sure that our target man had somehow got wind of it, which wouldn't be surprising if he was a local guy, as we thought he was. It was noticeable that no more attacks happened during this time. Sam argued for one more try and then let it rest until and unless the guy tried again, and I reflected that we might at least have frightened the bastard off, though he might just have moved territory.

So, like a late night matinee when you're already knackered, the show went on. I became a lady of the street with my usual professional care for detail – I'm a bona fide drag artiste, not a slap and mince karaoke queen, thank you very much. I patrolled Darrington Street with a carefully observed air of strolling about, while occasionally leaning up against a back wall and watching the world go by.

I was just meditating on whether boredom or hypothermia would drive me indoors first when the most enormous clout took me across the earhole, so hard and vicious that it made me stagger for a moment. I tried to turn and face the source of it, but there were more and more slaps and punches, slaps to the head, punches to the body. I did what I'd done ever since school in similar situations, and put my arms over my head to take what was coming until the strategic moment came for me to strike back, but I was conscious of being a bit groggy. I had the impression of a powerful but not particularly tall man, and for all he seemed to be wearing both scarf and cap, the cap pulled down, I saw a flash of grey at the temple which suggested this was no kid.

I had an idea "made a plan" is far too grand a term for thinking quickly in such circumstances – that going down on my knees might encourage him to come closer so that he could get on with doing what he wanted to do. It worked, in so far as he was hovering above me in seconds, and his crucial area was right in front of my forehead. The fact that he was getting off on this was visibly obvious. I pulled my head right back away from an intended big slap to the temple and then drove my forehead directly into his doodahs with a good deal of force and intention; like I said, I'd been here before, and these are not fights by Queensberry Rules. He sank down as I was getting up, which enabled me to swing a knee round into his head.

There we both paused for a few seconds. I'd pressed my alarm as soon as I felt a blow, and I knew several guys would already have emerged from well-concealed parts of the street; this wasn't a time for *dah-dah, dah-dah* sirens driving him off.

He was gasping and spitting a bit; he looked up at me with fire in his eyes, though still I could see the little flecks of grey under his cap. I could see in his eyes that he'd worked out something was badly wrong, from his point of view, from the size and strength of my blows. Somehow, he got to his feet and started making himself scarce, and now I could see why he could suddenly appear on the street; an open manhole, which at night no-one would see because it was well-shadowed by the side of a tall brick building, and who noticed closed manholes anyway? He'd had enough of me; he somehow got half way up and started for it, and I thought, how appropriate is this, he's like a rat from the sewer.

I knew if he made it down there, he'd be away again, and he only had about twenty feet to go. Even if I fancied the idea of following him down into the sewers, which I didn't, it was presumably territory he knew, or at least knew a lot better than I did. It was time to bring my rugby skills into play, and I daresay a few eyebrows will be raised at that –'rugby, Rox, really?' You bet your ass really; you tell me any other activities in school life where you can wrap your arms right round naked male thighs, fondle male bums and even give and receive a little doodah squeezing in the scrums, and they would have been on my extra-curricular list as well. Another form of bare thigh fondling is the tackle, and though this guy's thighs were currently trousered, I was ready to give it a go.

I launched myself over at him, my head and torso still feeling distinctly battered, and brought him down about six feet short of his precious escape hole. I could hear loud footsteps getting close. We both managed to get up as far as our knees, then we started swinging fists and arms at each other like two kids having a pillow fight. He caught me with some force just next to the chin; the world went blank, I closed my eyes, and I thought that was that for me, and then a fast, slim figure went past on my left and I forced my eyes open again to see Sam the policeman fetch the guy one of the finest right hooks I've ever seen – Sam had been storing that one up for a while, I reckon.

The guy's name was Eddie Latham, variously known to his workmates as Ed Case or the Drain Brain, and he'd worked for years down in the sewers, cleaning, maintenance, engineering, taking every opportunity he could, through grills, windows, glass roofs, whatever, to peer up at women and even take some footage on his mobile. Bit of a joke amongst the guys down there, until women were starting to complain and some of Ed's management team, two of them also women, got wind of what was going on and Ed was on his bike. Like guys do who get themselves into deep doodoo over women, or more accurately their attitudes to women, Ed turned his victims into his oppressors, and even though he was in his forties, he got himself into a security outfit and worked out to keep in shape, mostly so that he could lay about the women who he considered had caused him to be sacked. He had the same exhaustive Knowledge of the sewers as city taxi drivers have of the streets; he knew where to go in and where to come out, how he could get about without being waist deep in muck and water, and which parts of the system would be quiet and when. An educated rat, prowling underground to burst out on the attack when it suited him. The last attack before mine had given him jitters, and he'd left the area for a while, but the temptation to have another go was too strong. With countless witnesses against him, including me, he went down for long enough to make sure he wouldn't be bothering our girls again.

Witnessing meant that it couldn't be kept away from the media, of course. So I became an official hero and the act went even better; I started getting a few acting parts and panto work on the strength of it. It's a strange irony that it took a toerag attacking women to break me into something like a serious acting career, but that's showbiz.

What blew me away even more than my newfound heroism was when Dave Sorrell came and told me I had a new dressing room. At first, I was thinking, if it's a cubicle in the men's loo, I'm going to pack in drag and head off for my first Oscar, but then he took me to one of the Club's basement rooms, mostly dark and dusty and used for storing stuff, and I walked in to find myself in a big room the size of an upmarket bedsit, and I've done a few of them in my time – the bedsits, not the upmarket. Walk in shower, huge dressing mirror, wardrobe, and even a decent-sized bed.

'Rox,' he said, 'we don't ever want you to ever have to wander out into the night again after your performance. I heard about the boys, and the grapevine says it wasn't the first time. Sleep here, shower here, dress here, have your fans in, whatever.'

I was almost blubbing by this stage, and he went on to cover both of our embarrassments.

'We had to tank it,' – I hadn't the faintest idea what he was talking about, but it sounded impressive – 'drain it, ventilate it, what have you, but we got there.'

A curious thought stopped me blarting for a moment. Very sweet, yes, absolutely, but Dave Sorrell was legendarily as tight as an amphibious creature's posterior.

'This can't have come cheap, Dave. All out of your pocket?'

'Some,' he said, looking a bit shifty, like he does. 'But the girls chipped in, and there was a handsome contribution from – well, let's call it the Police Benevolent Fund.'

So there it is. Sam comes round now and then for a chat, the act continues and might even continue me into a real acting career, and Rox is the talk of the town. You can say what you like about manholes, decent and otherwise. Personally, I'm all for them.

Poems by David Crann

Just another suicide bomb

Out of a terracotta sky
a terracotta sun painted
the dwellings, suks and
dreaming minarets
in slabs of blood.

Our bloodshot eyes met.
Our faces, unusually bleached,
took on the aspect of raw meat.

Gobs and particles of insulted flesh
peppered us in bright red hail,
haphazard crimson meteors.

This had been our last day –
only echoing screams;
and the echo of the echoes.

The ground opened
to graves already cut:
and we were falling.
And we were falling...
a near infinity of waiting
yet no time to forgive
or not forgive, or calculate
where all the spades had come from...

Peace might come later,
blood paling to a rosier shade
of grey. Meantime, prayers blushed
and the augurs winked.

children of wars: j'accuse...

they are conceived
in ditch-dykes among munitions,
mortar shells and casings –
rusty, raw, and ragged
lethal blots: sperm, a brand
snatched from the fire
of blood-mud faecal filth;
a coagulating lava
to give these oblivions life…

they are delivered,
toboggans on a cresta run
on razored ice-blocks,
with a third-aid of white-hot,
blue-cold blunt incisions
from agricultural implements
of a signal savagery
and Neanderthal throwback –
plough-lancets
to sighs of scythes…

they are nourished
at barbed-wire breasts
and a cracked catastrophe
of nipple: milk trickles
in rancid heaps
to bloodied mucky gums…

these darling ragamuffins,
eyes bursting through bluebottles,
fix you blame:
conceived, delivered and nourished –
already halfway dead;
certificated, signed and sealed –
they fix you blame…
and all we do is watch…

Girl Soldiers – Equal Opportunities for post traumatic stress

[24th January 2013: The Pentagon lifts its ban forbidding female military personnel to serve on the front line in combat situations.]

She inhabits her very own personalised wasteland
whose illusion of infinity is punctured
by a limitless ring of ever-closing doors
and the turning of keys in revolving locks.

Hers is an emptiness no light or sound penetrates,
where her soul is drowning and her heart bleeds out.
Access to her brain is safeguarded by a maximum security password
she has inconveniently forgotten. Her memories spit out
random electronic measures of undigested slabs
of lumpy gravy. A prismatic fish gillie-spiked thrashes and splashes
on the water's edge, one eye glaring at the sun,
the other burrowing insanely in the sand.

She has abandoned her moccasins, her weapon and her war-bonnet
to the desert. She has been repatriated. She has received
state of the art military medical care and the congressional medal
for valour. Her family and her country are proud of her.

It would be unkind to describe her as a shadow. She is a corpse
refusing the gift of death. She is hooked to no life-support machine
that might conveniently be switched off. She is a soldier-girl
and has joined a happy band of equals.

Move her into the sun so that we might persuade ourselves
to believe that she feels its warmth; that she breathes in the fragility
of the honeysuckle and the yellow rose; that she basks
in the maudlin requiem of the whippoorwill.

David Crann

Leucothea

by Emma J Myatt

I

'The sea is biting cold. I am cumbersome with all the equipment; using a dry suit requires more of everything, especially strength. I'm thigh deep in the sea, tiny tears in the neoprene allowing arctic water to creep into my bubble. I shiver, wishing I'd checked the suit more carefully before remembering that it doesn't matter.

I wade out in my fins until I'm waist deep. My mask is still around my neck and I fit it over my eyes and nose. I put the regulator in my mouth and breathe the cool air, feeling my lungs fill in a way they don't on land. I wade deeper, the rocks becoming slippery with seaweed. As the water is about to close over my head, I notice a boat on the horizon. People out fishing? Have they seen me? Nobody is supposed to dive alone. I have a very good reason for doing it but I'm not about to explain it to anyone.

I duck quickly and the cold closing over my head makes me gasp for breath. My chest tightens and I can't breathe properly. I begin a count in my head to slow things down, until I've got myself under control. I let some air out of my jacket and feel myself sink more heavily onto the seabed with each step.

I check my air and depth gauges: everything's in order. I've enough air for about forty-five minutes, which is plenty. I let myself fall forwards, clear my ears and swim horizontally. I imagine myself Leucothea, feeling my body moving the way a sea spirit would. I clear my ears again and tune into the underwater clicks and whooshes, disconnecting myself from the world above.

This is my element. Always has been.

I'm gliding above the rocks, letting the current carry me along. Seaweed sways below me. I hear myself singing my diving tune; a song I always find in my mind when underwater. I am suddenly so grateful for this last experience of life that my eyes sting and fill. I blink rapidly to push the tears back because I can't lose it now. I concentrate instead on keeping the pressure in my ears equalised.

At twenty metres the water is clearer and a deep solid blue. A final checklist runs through my head: notes, all addressed and ready; car, left open with notes inside; house, everything in order; will, written. The relief I feel, combined with the weightlessness ignites a happiness within me and I stretch out my arms and soar, turn on my back and see the sun shimmering on the surface of the water way above. A few sunbeams break through and flicker towards me until they dissipate to nothing. The boat is long gone and I'm all alone again.

I turn back to face the seabed once more and begin searching for the wreck. Once past that, I know there's a deep trench. I check my depth and air and see that I'm close to the halfway mark, the point at which I could still turn back, have time for a decompression stop and surface with air still in my tank, as all good divers do. I let go of the gauge and promise myself it's the last time I shall look at it, until the deep blue of the trench is all around me and above me and I am safe.

The wreck looms before me like a live thing, seeming to drift closer as if it is me that's still. My breath catches. I swim close to it and lay a gloved hand on the rotting hull, seeing how it is becoming part of the sea. Eventually it'll relax down to nothing, sigh itself into the seabed. I pull myself up to the deck. It's lop-sided and broken. Fish glimmer everywhere, bringing the dead boat to life. I see an eel peer out at me from a rusty hole.

Something catches my eye in the old wheelhouse. I look up but whatever-it-was has gone, all I see is the flick of a large greenish tail, disappearing behind the boat. A seal? Porpoise? Usually they're more curious than afraid.

I swim on, kicking and pushing myself over the wreck and down the other side, towards the trench. I see it immediately, a jagged hole in the rocks, which widens and stretches until it looks as if the seabed is trying to tear itself in half. I kick harder and let myself glide over it until the edges are too far apart for me to see, all is blue and dark. That beautiful depth. My ears hurt and I have to kick upwards slightly to clear them, before going down once more.

I stretch out my arms and legs again and allow myself to float down, taking nothing but the desire to be free. I can feel the heaviness inside me lifting. The guilt is ebbing away after months. I'm paying back what it was I took. I give in to the feeling of freedom, dimly aware that my air is getting harder to suck. My ears are sore again, but it doesn't matter. I have a go at clearing them and they pop a little.

I am letting go.

Something darts across my field of vision. A large animal – dolphin? The seal again? It briefly rouses me from the warm contentment which is spreading as I descend.

'Go back,' sings a voice. Is it in my head? It's in my head. It's my life force (never my soul) urging me one last time not to give up. I expected this, I expected a bit of fight from something deep down within me. 'You don't belong here, Laura, go *back*,' the voice is insistent, no longer singing. And it knows my name.

And suddenly there is a face in front of me. Part of me knows I must be looking at a seal; they are curious and she'll be wondering what I'm doing in her world, but it's such a human face that for a second I am angry. I wanted to be alone. I reach out and push it away and I see sorrow cross the curiosity in the eyes. Then the face is gone with a silky flick of movement.

My air is nearly gone. I can still manage little sips, but soon there will be none. Then suddenly, it's gone. I let the regulator fall from my lips and close my eyes, seeing red against blue, a flower of death bursting out into the water. I open my mouth and in rushes the cold heavy water. I feel it going down my throat. I welcome it.

And then there is a mouth on mine. A soft, cool mouth. I open my eyes and see green irises before me, hair flowing around us. And I feel myself being pulled and pushed upwards.'

I finish reading. I can never tell the man in front of me how I long to be back there. 'You were very lucky that those fishermen found you. *Incredibly* lucky there was a decompression chamber close by,' Dr Collins says.

'Yes,' I say, still unable to forget the green eyes.

'You wrote this in the present tense,' the doctor says, indicating my statement. He calls it a Cleansing Piece, all the suicidal ones had to write them about how we didn't die. And we have to keep reading them aloud. It doesn't help, but he thinks it does. I suppose he wants to see my reaction to it one last time before he decides my fate.

I'm not sure how to respond to this so I say nothing. But I think, it's because I've never surfaced.

'Laura? You understand why I'm asking?' He's said all of this before.

'Yes, I did. It felt very real. But I know it wasn't. It was just hallucinations brought on by the narcs. I mean nitrogen narcosis.'

'How do you feel about it now?'

'It wasn't real, and I'm aware of that now. I no longer feel suicidal and I look forward very much to going home and starting again. I can't believe how stupid I was. Guilt makes you do funny things.' He has to believe me; I can't stay within these pale yellow walls another day.

'So you don't feel guilty now?'

'Yes, I do, but I will make amends in other ways. I no longer feel I have to pay the world back with my own life.'

'Strictly speaking Laura, it *wasn't* your fault, as we've discussed many times. You are in the clear.' Dr Collins leans back in his chair.

In the clear. Strange words. Of course, the man in front of me can't see the mess of bodies in the shallows; the crimson blood as it blooms out into the clear blue; he can't hear the screaming; see the shocked faces; the broken deck chairs, the speedboat forced way out of its element onto the sand. He didn't find himself waking up in the cockpit to all that, the creeping horror of realising it was All. My. Fault. I see it all, every day. I know how it ends, every time.

'And I'm feeling good about that. Like I said, I look forward to starting again,' I say, looking at him, unblinking.

There's a silence which stretches and I'm worried, before he leans forward and tells me I'll be under observation and that there are conditions but all I really listen to is "leaving us" so inside I'm rejoicing.

There are awkward goodbyes then I exit the building and walk to the bus stop. I've made sure nobody is there to meet me. They kept telling me it wasn't my fault but I saw the way nobody could look me in the eye afterwards; felt the way I could silence a room just by entering it. My job was the only blessing, sitting alone in my office, writing reports about the state of the sea, diving whenever I could, before I realised I didn't deserve a place in the world any more.

I scan the bus timetable. There's only one place I can go and I notice with satisfaction that the right bus will be here in just a few minutes. What I'm doing is right, then. It's a sign. I let my bag fall to the pavement next to me and turn so my face is in the sun. I close my eyes.

Which is a mistake because immediately I see red against blue, life bleeding out into the water. Horror-stricken faces, a twisted deckchair flung up the beach.

I open my eyes again. It'll never go away. And if it ever does, then I have no right to be alive. I should not even have been *in* the boat that day due to my back injury but I hadn't wanted to miss the beach party, our end of project celebration.

The bus arrives and I get on, pay the driver some money, feel my breath hitch in my throat in case he can see my thoughts as he looks at me and smiles. He lets me on. There are only a few people on the bus and I'm sure nobody has noticed me. Life outside glides past, wobbling slightly through the dirty glass as if we were all underwater.

I think about the green eyes staring into mine. The eyes that knew everything but were still wrong. That was exactly where I belonged. I wish that *thing* had let me stay. What awaits me now is a dead life, if that is possible. A life of deadness. Deathlife. A living death? I've never agreed with myself how to describe what it's going to be.

Cranmore House, the place they've told me I'll stay for a while "until I get back on my feet" will by now have been informed I'm coming and if I'm late they'll come out looking for me. I will the lumbering bus to go faster.

I watch other people's lives drift past: dog-walkers shoppers street cleaners toddlers toddling cats jumping garden walls containing flowers women chatting drunk men staggering from the pub smoking pushchairs casually held in one hand rolling people eating man running a policeman talking to an old woman girl cycling. All of it, all going on all of the time. The minutiae of life. A million tiny events every second. In any moment, all of it could be taken away. The bus driver could have a heart attack and crash through those school gates; that red car could have a blowout and pin the cyclist against the wall; the mother who's chatting on her mobile could let go of her child's hand for an instant and the child could run in front of the bus.

I suddenly feel sick. When my thoughts start spinning like this I find it hard to hold on to what's real. As if any of it is!

I will the bus to move faster and miraculously it does, everything speeds up and it's my stop and I get off leaving my bag exactly where it is and bolt for the doors and ignore the shout behind me and make for the right street and run up the hill and see the sign saying *Fosse Cliff* and feel the pull of the sea tugging me ever forwards, drawing me in until I can hear the gulls and see the massive blue stretching out before me and I'm at the top and I don't know exactly how I got here but here I am and here is the only place I was ever really headed.

I breathe. I stretch out my arms and just like I do when I'm underwater, I gently let myself fall forwards.

II

Ray gets a couple of extra minutes this morning before it hits him with a nauseating flip in his abdomen, the little reminder that it isn't all a dream. Usually it gets him right away, but this morning he lies half-asleep listening to Win humming in the shower, thinks about her soft warm body and rolls onto her side of the bed, to lie on her pillow and smell her night cream. As he does every day, he thanks whatever it was that brought her to him and filled up his aloneness and made him laugh. Then he remembers It, all over again, and it's all spoiled.

He checks his left leg; it's the same as it has been all week since it got a little worse – perhaps slightly stiffer. It's hard to tell. He makes a fist with his right hand and smiles slightly; it feels a bit better. Maybe. He does struggle to decide sometimes – if he's feeling rough in his head his whole body feels wrong. If he feels good, if he's having one of those random days full of joy like he did yesterday, he feels better all over and can kid himself he's going to beat It.

Win's still humming and splashing so he opens his bedside drawer, reaches right to the back, to the old cigar box he's had since he was a child, pulls it out and lifts the lid. There they are, next to the leaflets full of support group numbers and information about It, the little pills that the doctor says will help, will delay the onset of symptoms. He pushes two out and dry-swallows them. The shower stops so he shuts the box and shoves it back in, closing the drawer. He tries to remember when his next appointment is. It's perhaps sometime this week. He'll have to phone and check, which he always has to do seeing as he can't write it down on the calendar. Win would keep him right, of course, which is probably a good reason to tell her, just as good as the reason that if he doesn't, she'll probably leave him. I'll never lie to you, he'd said, when she'd told him about John, her ex. She'd fixed him with her deep blue eyes and said, No, Ray, I don't believe you would. It took him less than two years to begin hiding stuff from her and he knows, just as he knows that you don't get a gift in life without getting an equal amount of good stuff taken away, that she will not forgive him when she finds out. If she finds out.

'Morning Raymond,' says Win as she emerges from the bathroom in a cloud of steam.

'Morning Winifred,' he replies, winking and placing onto his face a bright smile. 'Sleep well?'

'Til you snored. And you must've been dreaming because you kept twitching. Your left leg kept kicking me. Were you dreaming about footie?'

Ray looks at her and frowns, feeling a cold ball settle into his stomach. 'No, no I wasn't. I'll get up,' he says.

But Win's already bustling out of the room, still in her towel, calling over her shoulder, 'Stay and relax, you're not working til eleven today. I'll get you the paper and a coffee.'

'Win–' he starts, but she's gone. He stares at the space where she just was. 'I don't deserve you,' he whispers. He lifts back the covers and looks at his leg. Twitching isn't good. Twitching at night, when he doesn't even know – that's worse than not good. He feels sick. He holds out both his hands. Are they shaking? His right hand looks like it is. He makes two fists and slams them down on the bed, either side of him. If the shakes start, it's bye bye bus, bye bye life and probably, bye bye Win. And losing Win would be the end. If they'd not been married when he got diagnosed, he'd have told her. The fact that it came a month after his wedding – one month! – had just thrown him. He shakes his head and is still shaking it when Win walks in, his coffee in one hand and the other holding the paper close up to her face. She's saying something about it being a terrible shame.

'What's that, love?' he asks, mostly to divert his thoughts. He doesn't really want to know at all – no more bad news – but she's reading it.

'I've not got my specs on but looks like someone's thrown themselves off the cliffs. A girl.'

'I don't–'

'Oh my god, says here she got off the Number 43 bus – isn't that yours? – and they're looking for people who might've seen her before... Wait til I get my specs.'

Ray grabs the paper and stares at the photograph on the front page. He recognises her straight away. She looks younger in the photograph, wild black curly hair down to her shoulders, a big open smile on her face and her eyes, wide and full of life, smiling as much as her mouth. Ray remembers faces. Yesterday she hadn't looked like that. He'd noticed her because she hadn't looked right and he remembers thinking, man trouble? She hadn't looked directly at him but he'd seen her eyes – they were dull and the whites were red. And the way she'd got off –

'Ray?'

'Oh, God,' he says. The way she got off, she'd left her bags and run and with a thud in his middle he remembers the stop they were at when she ran. He puts his hand to his forehead. 'She got off by Fosse Road, the nearest place to Fosse Cliff. Jesus. She got off, running, left her bags and ignored me when I shouted after her and ran in front of the bus and across the road. I was angry. I looked round and saw her stuff there and thought about how she'd ignored me and I felt angry. I let her go. I closed the doors because I was late and I drove off. And I didn't think about her much, even when I had to take her bags in at the end of the route and get them booked. Shit. Shit, shit *shit.*' He puts his hand over his mouth.

The bed creaks as Win sits next to him and looks over his shoulder. They both read:

CLIFF DEATH
by Tamsin Brown

Yesterday morning a young woman – who has been named locally as Laura Jones – fell to her death from the top of Fosse Cliff. Miss Jones, 31, had been under observation at Hallmead Hospital after a suicide attempt last year. She left the hospital yesterday morning on the (Number 43) bus after being discharged to travel to a nearby supported living environment. It is understood that on the way there Miss Jones walked to the top of Fosse Cliff where she then fell to her death. There are not believed to be any suspicious circumstances. The police have asked anyone – especially those on the same bus – who may have seen Laura Jones yesterday to contact them as soon as possible on 0865 5500 500. Miss Jones' family have been informed. ***More on page 4****.*

Ray doesn't speak but finds the right page.

Continued from front page
Last year the ***Echo*** *reported that Laura Jones had been involved in an accident which claimed the lives of four people, including one child. Miss Jones was taking strong painkillers for back pain and was driving a speedboat just off Fosse Sands when she fell asleep and the boat collided with two families on the beach. Miss Jones reportedly had not been informed she should not operate any machinery while taking the medication and she did not know what the side-effects could be.*

According to one of her friends whom the ***Echo*** *interviewed at the time, Miss Jones tried to end her life because she could not live with the sense of guilt she felt. According to one source the doctor who prescribed the medication has been under investigation about the incident.*

‘I’ll have to call them,’ Ray says.

Win takes his hand. ‘If it was suicide, she probably made her mind up a long time before.’ Her voice is gentle, careful.

Ray says nothing. He is remembering a time when he sat in his car, at the top of a hill on the way to Portsmouth and wondered how much hosepipe he’d need. He’d just left the doctor’s where he’d gone for a follow up appointment after being told the stiffness was probably repetitive strain injury after driving for so many years, but they’d give him these tests *just in case* so in he walked expecting to be told he’d need a bit of time off work, perhaps some physio and then *Wham*, in a few seconds everything was different. He’d sat in his car for six hours, thought about ways it could be done, wondered if he had the guts and decided he had, if not for Win. They still had leftover wedding cake at home. Hadn’t even got all the honeymoon pictures printed. So he drove to the pub, ditched the car and got drunk and when he got home, Win was angry for a while but he hadn’t had to tell her and after that first day it got easier not to.

He looks at her now. ‘I’m going to get a shower then I’ll call them. I don’t think I’ll go to work today. I’ll call Mike and get cover. I don’t think I’d be safe.’ He looks at the time. ‘Don’t be late for work, I know you’ve got that day trip today.’

‘It’s okay, I can stay a bit longer. The oldies can wait a little while.’

‘Honest, Win, I’m fine. You go. They’ve probably been looking forward to it all week.’ He manages a smile.

‘If you’re sure you’re alright…’

‘I’m all right. It’s a shock, to be sure. I should have… I wish… Oh hell, I don’t know. Maybe she didn’t kill herself.’ But he remembers the sadness he’d thought was man trouble in her and thought, she did mean to. I just didn’t realise it. He’d been happy yesterday, he remembers that. All around were folk getting on with their lives as he drove; he’d felt as if he was driving through a beautiful picture, with tiny important details of life being played out all around him and he was in the middle of it with all these people’s lives literally in his hands and he’d felt strong and safe and *happy*. It had been a gift day, a truly happy day when he usually had It hanging over him too much to do anything except pretend.

He’d had all those people’s lives in his hands including Laura Jones’s. He shrugs off this thought so Win doesn’t see it and kisses her. ‘Go, I’ll see you tonight. Fancy an Indian?’

He holds it together until he hears the front door close and then he holds his face in his hands and sobs.

After his shower he feels able to call work and the police, with whom he arranges an interview in the afternoon.

He thinks of Win, pushing wheelchairs around the garden centre, holding papery hands and helping old ladies choose plants. He tries to imagine her pushing him around in a chair, or walking next to him as he rides a mobility scooter. Shame makes him close his eyes. It could be years before you lose your mobility, could be years before it gets really bad, the doctors had said. But he knows different. Those little pills that hide under the leaflets are not helping. The symptoms are only getting worse and this is not a good sign, he knows it. He tries to push away the truth because if he thinks about it too much, and stops telling the doctor, 'No, no worse at all!' then he might as well have bought the hosepipe after all because it's all going to end really soon anyway. Those pills are his religion. If he stops believing in them, he has nothing.

He opens the bedside drawer again and takes out the cigar box. He opens it and pulls out the leaflets that have been folded up in there for the last fourteen months. The first one he opens is numbers for support groups. Apparently there are lots; all, if he believes the pictures, attended by happy, hand-holding couples smiling into the camera as if to say, 'Yeah, I've got Parkinson's but it's great! Look at us! Look how happy we are!'

He knows what Win would have done by now, called every single one and taken him there and met people and got him involved and he would have gone, to please her, because he'd do anything to please her. All he wants is to make her happy and all she says she wants is to be with him. But now? As if she is right there in the room, he hears her voice in his head. Raymond Baillie, do you honestly think that would make any difference to me? Don't you remember our wedding vows? I love you, and I'm here for you whatever happens. Do you really think I'd leave you? Be ashamed of you? Think you less of a man?

And suddenly something in him shifts. He feels on the brink of an understanding. He breathes, and lets it come. First comes the knowledge that he has to tell her because she deserves to know and she is the best friend he's been waiting for his whole life, all fifty-two years of it. When he's not with her it's like half of him is missing. How has he thought it was alright *not* to tell her? How has he even considered it was okay to try and cope with this on his own?

'What have I been *doing*?' he says. He looks again at the picture of the girl from the bus, and then he knows, all of a sudden he knows, what he has to do. He thinks about her eyes and imagines what she was holding inside her – the lives of four other people.

He imagines himself driving his bus, pushing the truth deep down inside him until even *he* doubts it's there, hiding it and hiding it until one day his body literally stops working and he suddenly cannot steer and there is a car coming the other way around a corner, a car full of a family and the bus goes straight into them.

'There but for the grace of God go I,' he whispers, and he picks up the phone.

III

Ray? It's me.

I'm going to be late home.

No, go ahead and eat, I can warm mine.

I can't explain now, but I need to be here.

Sorry?

About what? Can it wait until later?

Alright. Yes, I love you too. See you later tonight.

This isn't heaven. I know that voice, it's Winnie, one of the volunteers. She's standing by the edge of my bed. This is not my bed! This is the bloody hospital. They've brought me back, again! It's in my notes, *DO NOT RESUSCITATE*, clear as day. Why won't they just let me go? I'm ready – more than ready. I've had my life and it's been good and now I'm just taking up space. Let me go and see Maud.

'Why won't they just let me go?' My voice doesn't sound right.

'Frank? Welcome back.'

Winnie's bending over me, smiling. 'I said, why –'

'Don't try to speak, let me get a nurse.' And she's gone.

I look around me. My head's awful stiff and it feels like it's stuffed with sawdust. I know what's happened though, I remember it all. No memory loss, like last time when I woke up and had no idea of anything. We was at the garden centre. Winnie was helping me choose something for David for his birthday and then I felt it coming on me and Winnie helped me sit down and I thought, this is it, Franky-boy, this is where you leave the world. And I smiled at Winnie, I remember that, and then here I am. So I guess it's me heart again, and they've zapped me back to life with those paddle things and I'm back. Again.

Winnie reappears with the nurse.

'Yes, just after you left, I heard him saying something.'

'Mr Willis? Can you hear me?' The nurse is loud.

'I'm not bloody deaf,' I tell her and see Winnie smothering a smile behind her hand. I give her a wink. She's all right, is Winnie.

'You're in A and E. You collapsed at the garden centre. Do you remember?' Winnie speaks around the nurse, who looks a little annoyed.

'Yep. Me heart, I'm guessing?'

'Actually, they don't think so. Not this time. You collapsed and we called an ambulance, but you were all right – I mean your heart was working fine, you were breathing, just unconscious. They said your blood pressure is really low and –'

'Thank you, would you mind waiting outside for a moment? I just need to check a few things with Mr Willis.' And before Winnie can object, the nurse is shutting the curtains around me right in front of Winnie so she has to step back.

'Oh,' she says. 'I'll be just outside, Frank.'

The nurse speaks to me as if I'm seven, prods and pokes and shines stuff in my eyes all efficient like but then gives me a kindly smile. Maybe she's okay. 'A doctor will be along to see you soon. You're probably going to have to spend the night here,' she says.

'Thanks,' I say. I'm not feeling all that thankful though to tell the truth. Body hurts, I'm so old people most don't see me anymore, my family don't visit. It's time for me to go, like I said. The nurse squeaks off across the shiny floor and a few moments later Winnie reappears. Winnie's one of the folk who still sees me. She often tells me I'm her favourite at the Inverluthe Daycare. *Daycare.* Makes us sound like children.

'You don't need to stay,' I tell Winnie.

'I'll stay til you get a proper bed, or they chuck me out. It's fine. I've rung Ray and he's fine. We didn't really have plans tonight and even if we did, I'm not passing up an opportunity to spend an evening with my favourite man.'

'If I knew you wasn't joking I'd tell that man of yours,' I say.

'Oh he's fine. He doesn't mind sharing me,' she says and winks. 'Now. If you're here for the night I can ring one of the others at the centre and get them to pop home for you? Doesn't your neighbour have a key?'

'Mrs Sharman. Yes, she does.'

'How do you feel?' Winnie takes my hand in hers.

I consider for a moment. 'I'm tired, my body's worn out, I think my time should be up. Let someone else have a go. I don't think the end's too far away.'

Winnie looks upset again. 'But you're still young, mentally, and compared to some at Inverluthe, you're a spring chicken!'

'*Sprung* chicken, maybe. What's that saying – had a hard paper round?'

Winnie laughs. 'Yeah, that's the saying. You were a fisherman weren't you?'

'Yes. Just up the coast. Used to fish these waters too, sometimes. Loads more fish back in the day. All gone now and all these bloody quotas – so much gets wasted! It's a crime. We knew, us folk back then knew how to keep the oceans happy. We cared for them. We threw back tiddlers, we didn't use those dragging nets they use now… It was a different world.'

'You're not wrong there,' says Winnie.

I've got a story inside me I've never told anyone. And if I'd died today, it would've died too. I think it should be told. Winnie's a good listener. But would she believe me?

'While we're on the subject… Would you mind if I told you a story?'

Winnie looks around the bits of the ward we can see. It's busy. 'Don't think anyone's going to come anytime soon,' she says. 'I'd love to hear a story.'

'It's a true story,' I say. I wonder where to start. I've never told a soul. Don't know why. Just never found the right time. And, just like I had that thought a second ago, another thought pops into my head like someone else has put it there. I *have* to tell her, right now.

'Would you pass me my jacket?' I say.

Winnie turns to the pile of folded clothes with my jacket placed neatly on top. She puts it in front of me. I reach to the inside pocket and take out a small drawstring bag, made of green velvet. I hold it in my right hand and close my fist over it. Although I've held it every day for the last fifty years, it always gives me a slight sort of jolt. Like it's alive a little bit. This is probably why I've never told anyone the story.

'Maybe I shouldn't, after all,' I say and Winnie nods.

'Okay. Whatever you want. But some things just have to be told. I need to tell my Ray that, he's holding back a story from me, I know it. He'll tell me when he's ready, I know that as well. Telling things makes them real.'

It's this that decides me. She's right, nothing is real if it's stored in your head. Telling it gives it life I suppose.

'Right,' I begin. 'This story is fifty years old and I never even told Maud. I wish I had. Still hope to be able to if we end up in the same place. You religious, Winnie?'

She shrugs. 'Some days I am. Others not. I think if there was a god he'd not let half the stuff that happens, happen. But there's too much *stuff* out there for there not to be *something*. So, not sure. What about you?'

'I think there's a god. But not like any god we talk about. This god's a dangerous, dark bloke who is as much about war as he is about peace. See, you can't have one without the other, can you? But I believe in heaven, and hell. Hope I go wherever Maud's gone.' I pause. Been thinking about her an awful lot, lately. She's been gone nearly seven years. I'm fed up of being alone.

'I was a fisherman up the coast. Like I told you. Fished for whatever we could get and sold it at the market. Maud was a teacher at the local school and we did well. She used to come out and help me during the holidays. Sometimes I'd take other blokes out to help, sometimes it was just me. There's a small island off the coast about five miles north of Fosse Bay near where we used to drop our lobster and crab pots. If I had time I'd pull the boat onto the beach and walk a little. The island's still there but it's got buildings on it now; they've made a bird-watching research thing out there. Back then though, it was deserted. Got real peace out there. I loved the family but with four young kids it was pretty noisy. Fishermen get used to solitude, you know? So sometimes I'd stay a bit longer than I should and just sit, and watch the waves.' Those were fine days. I felt glad to be alive, glad to be a fisherman. Glad of God, whatever he was, for making all of it. I smile at the memory of myself, young and strong, resting on that beach.

I reach for a sip of water but Winnie's there already, passing me the glass. I see my hand shaking a bit as I tip it towards me. Winnie's kind hand closes over my own and helps guide it to my lips. I have a long drink and lay back for a moment.

'You're a good un,' I tell her. 'Ray's lucky.'

'So I keep telling him. Only if he behaves, though! Fancy, all this love at our age.'

'Shush woman. You've got thirty years on me. Plenty life left.'

'I hope so. Me and Ray have a lot of plans.'

'It goes quick, but you can fill it up and make it slow down,' I say.

'So, you're on the island…?' Winnie prompts me.

'I'm on the island. That island. Was my own bit of paradise. Never took anyone there and only a few folk used it for fishing so usually just me alone there. So, this day I'm lying on the beach watching the shags and the terns and the gulls. Thinking about jobs I needed to do to the boat, and the fact that Maud wanted me to take a holiday but it was the best season for fishing. I remember. I was looking at the rocks and suddenly it seemed like one moved. Rocks always look different – the light, the tides, the waves – you think you recognise them but they seem to change every day. I could've seen this one before. Wasn't sure. But it moved. I swear it. I watched harder. Nothing happened and I decided it was a trick of the light. But just as I moved my head, I saw it move again. This time I wasn't wrong, I was sure of it. So I gets up, and goes to have a look.' I can't help but chuckle, remembering.

'What?' asks Winnie.

'Telling this, it's strange. It's never been told but it's like the story wants to come out. You're going to think I'm nuts, though. Send me off up to Hallmead.'

'Frank, not much surprises me. Trust me, you're sane. That's not going to change.'

'Well, we'll see,' I say, flexing my hand around the green velvet bag. 'I walked over to the rock. It was like a normal rock every time I looked at it and I knew the beach pretty well and was sure it was a rock I'd seen before. Maybe. But every time I looked somewhere else, it kind've flickered. Shimmered. And then I looked back and it was just a rock. Thought I was seeing things.'

I could still stop, save Winnie's view of me as a nice sane old man. But she's listening so hard and anyway this story wants to be told. I can feel it. In my hand, the green velvet bag is warm.

'I walked right up to it and bent down. And I saw a face. Honest to God, I jumped back about five feet. I think I shouted something. From where I was, it was just a rock again but then I went closer and looked and looked and there it was again, a face. And it was in pain. How can I describe it? It looked a bit like a seal, and that's what I thought it was, a hurt seal stranded. But it had green eyes, bright green eyes and long hair which could be seaweed at first glance but I could now see was hair. And it was all curled up so the face was sort of tucked down below this, this *tail*, a shimmery, silvery-green dolphin tail. But not a dolphin tail, cause I've seen plenty of them. Well, I just stood there and stared. And these green eyes stared back. I dunno what possessed me then but I reached out and touched it. And this mouth appeared from nowhere and hissed at me! Like an angry snake. No words, just a hiss. And something snapped at me and I turned and ran.'

Winnie's looking at me like she's really interested.

'What happened next?' She's whispering.

'Well, I thought I was ill, seeing things, like. I turned towards my boat and started running. But then, I heard this call. This singing lonely call. It sounded like it was in pain. Sort of like a cat and a dog and a seal. Peculiar. I stopped dead and looked back at the rock thing, certain it'd come from there. There were no words but it was calling me back. Like I imagined a siren to sound. Singing to my soul.' I can't help it, the memory makes me shiver.

'So I went back. I was scared. Really scared. And aware I was all alone out there. But when I got back the thing had gone less rock-like. It was now a soft wet shiny *thing* like a seal, like a fish, like a – mermaid. No other word for it. But not a pretty mermaid like you see in kids' books. No, this was a frightening creature. It had green eyes and skin of all shades of blue, green and red. It seemed to change colour. It held my gaze with terrifying eyes then looked down at its tail and then I saw the nets. It was all tangled up with nets and wire. It was stuck.'

We stare at each other for a moment. Winnie looks like a wide-eyed child. She believes me, I see that right away and I'm relieved. We both turn at the squeaky sound of someone walking up the ward. A tall young man in greens is looking at me, the nurse by his side.

'We've found you a bed, Mr Willis,' the nurse says to me. 'Doctor Baldwin here just wants to do some tests before you leave this ward. Thanks for staying, but you can go home now,' she says to Winnie.

Winnie looks at me, and I say to the nurse, 'Please, could I have five more minutes? I'm giving Winnie here some directions to my house so she can bring me clothes.'

Winnie smiles brightly. The doctor is frowning. 'We'll be really quick,' says Winnie.

'All right. I have another patient to see here, which I can do first. But when I come back I really will have to ask you to–'

'It's okay, I'll be gone,' Winnie says. They both nod and walk away.

'What happened next?' Winnie leans forwards. 'Are you all right to continue?'

'I'm nearly at the end,' I say, and know it's true. 'Well. I squatted down – a bit nervous cause I'd seen this thing hiss and knew it had teeth but it needed help. And there was intelligence in the eyes. Like human intelligence but cold, so, so cold. I reached out my hands toward the net and nothing happened, no hissing. So I reached out both hands and tugged at the net a little. The creature gave a growl of pain and I knew this was

going to be difficult. The net was all twisted around and cutting into its skin. To make it short, in case that doctor comes back, I got out my knife and cut away all the net and stuff. The tide was coming in so I got wet but I didn't care. The creature didn't make a sound except these odd hisses when I hurt it accidentally. Eventually, I got all the net off. By this time I was kneeling in the water up to my neck. It tried to move its tail and although it must've hurt, it could move okay. It swam right up to me and put its face very close to mine, then it put a hand – I didn't even see its hands before – behind my neck and pulled me forwards, right under the water. Well, I thought I was a goner. I tried to push myself up but this thing was strong, much stronger than me. I could do nothing but be pulled forwards. We ended up in the water and I thought I was going to drown. But it put its face right up to mine again and I heard words in my head, Thank you, and something was pressed into my hand and I felt a slither next to me and then I was alone, face down in cold water, wondering what the hell had just happened.'

The telling of this has worn me out. I open my hand and hold out the green velvet bag to Winnie, who takes it. I see she's got tears in her eyes. I see she believes me. I smile. 'That's it.'

'Is this what it gave you?'

'That's what it gave me. Look inside.'

Winnie opens the bag and slides the stone into her palm. 'It's beautiful!'

'Isn't it,' I say. It's the colour of the creature's tail – all colours, flowing in and out of each other. It shimmers and shines and seems to glow, somehow. Winnie gazes at it.

'Take it,' I tell her.

'I can't, it's–'

'Soon after this happened, we had a tough time in the family. That's probably why I didn't tell Maud about what happened on the island. Long story, I'll not go there now. But this stone – this stone seemed to help me. It's got this kind of energy. Hold it. You'll see what I mean. It helped me. I don't need it anymore. It's right I should pass it on, and as nobody else knows the story, I feel you should have it. In case you ever need some help with anything. I used to sit and hold this and sort of feel recharged.'

She's trying to protest when the doctor comes back. I hand her the bag and she slips the stone in. 'I'll come and see you tomorrow,' she says. 'We can talk about it then.'

'Thank you,' I tell her. 'For listening to a mad old man.'

She leans over me and whispers in my ear, 'You're not mad. Thank you for the story,' and she gives me a soft kiss on my cheek. She turns, and she's gone. And so's the stone. I feel light. Like the water vapour that rises from the waves.

The Jouster

by Colin Heffernan

I got to know Jimmy in the hospital over a bucket of potato peels. I was there because I said the wrong thing to a pair of boots one night in the city. The boots got angry and they had to keep me in an induced coma for three months, until my brain fit my head again. I haven't been myself since. My doctors tell me it's because of damage to my prefrontal cortex. It doesn't feel like damage. It feels like a fog in which I'm going around in circles, almost finding the edges. My parents took me home when I was well enough, thinking I'd be good as new in no time, back to the insurance brokers I worked for, the Friday pints with the lads, the missus I'd been seeing on-and-off that they liked and hoped I'd make a go of it with. It was tough on them when I wasn't improving and I'd get into awful rages. The incident in the filling station was the end of it. After that, we all agreed the safest option for me was the hospital.

The main house is a tired building from which yellow paint peels constantly, as though the walls are producing the stuff. They'd have closed it long ago only for the lack of anywhere better to house us brain-bandaged idiots. We are a little community here, soothed by the mechanical routine of the place, by the automation of the people who provide our care. We are drugged at breakfast, lunch and dinner, our wits and whims dampened by a technicolour of pills and liquids. In the mornings we have jobs. I peel potatoes in the canteen kitchen. I would have hated that kind of work before my injury. Now it's calming, requiring no decisions, only repetition. The chefs call me Speedy on account of how slow I am at everything but I don't mind. I'm glad that there's something left of me to put a name on. The hospital grounds are nice, thick with evergreen forest in which I like to walk. In the evenings I sit on one of the rusting benches scattered amongst the trees and in the silence there I can put some order to my foggy thoughts. The days are short now. I have a wristwatch that squeals its alarm at me when the sunset is coming so that I don't stay too long. That used to happen before but not since my parents bought me the watch.

Jimmy started on a Wednesday, his head bowed down and lolling like a bobble-head toy, his cheap tracksuit hanging from him like he'd shrunk inside it. He waited at the kitchen door for direction, his eyes locked onto the turmeric-stained vinyl floor. The chefs put him on potatoes with me.

We sized each other up across the peels bucket as best we could, Jimmy unable to look at me while I could examine all I wanted without a clue what any of it meant.

'Name?' he asked in the same way that a doctor's secretary might.

'Alan,' I told him. 'You?'

'Jimmy. My friends call me the Jouster.'

'Why's that?'

'Age?'

'Twenty-six. You?'

'Almost the same.'

He peeled like a man under threat, turning the potatoes in nimble hands. What usually took me two hours was done in forty minutes and the chefs directed us to the stack of dirty roasting trays for the rest of the morning. I see the specialists in the afternoons, my psychiatrist, my occupational therapist and psychologist. They flirt with my broken head but it gives nothing back. The psychotherapist I meet with each week is a kind lady named Susan. I touched her leg during our first session and there was a bit of a drama about it but we've gotten on well since and she tells me I'm making progress. At night we watch movies. Dan, the new psychiatric nurse, downloads the recent releases to bring to work. He's been a real find. He brings news from the city and he can interpret it into our language. I haven't been there since the night I was hurt, except for the one excursion to Tivoli that led to the incident outside the Topaz. My parents offer to take me on home visits for a few hours, back to Glasheen where I grew up, the same mid-terrace they've lived in their whole lives. They only offer because they know I'm too scared to say yes.

The next day I noticed that Jimmy struggled to talk and work at the same time so I began to sabotage his progress, eager to avoid the roasting trays.

'Where'd you come from?'

His hands ground to a halt, his head wobbling on its neck. 'Duncree. A training centre for individuals with high-functioning autism. I am now FETAC-qualified in sheet metal fabrication. Thank you.'

'Special needs then.'

He exhaled through his nose and mouth simultaneously, a kind of slow-motion sneeze. 'I have difficulties with conversation, eye-contact, social decorum and stupid people. These are ordinary things. My needs are therefore ordinary.'

'Mine's a brain injury. I was attacked in the city.'

For the briefest instance, Jimmy looked at me. 'By what?'

'Boots.'

'Oh.'

An hour later I was scrubbing pans again.

'What were you thinking?' Susan asked that afternoon, always digging for better reasons than scar-tissue and swelling. 'Outside the petrol station, I mean.'

'I don't know.'

'Were you scared to go any closer to the city because of what happened there? Did you want someone to take that choice away from you?'

'I don't know.'

My head feels like a fishing reel spun into a mess after a bad cast and Susan thinks she can undo the knots but nobody has the hands for that job. On Friday Jimmy arrived wearing a cycling helmet that he'd spray-painted silver and fastened thin bits of sheet metal onto so that it looked like a knight's great-helm. He placed it on a coat-hook in the kitchen like it was his most prized thing. He went to use the toilet and the chefs laughed at him while he was gone. I couldn't handle another morning scrubbing so I decided to talk him useless.

'Why the helmet?'

'Protection.'

'From what?'

'From whatever's out there.' He flicked a glance at me again, a millisecond of eye-contact. 'The city's not a safe place. The CSO consistently reports that crime rates are inflated in the cities, particularly Dublin but also Cork. Considering its poor reputation, Limerick has a relatively low rate of crime but I don't live there so it hardly helps me. Did you know that?'

'What?'

'About higher crime-rates in the cities.'

'No.'

'Now you know that. Thank you.'

'Have you had problems?'

'Sometimes I come across pockets of resistance.'

'So you fight?'

'Yes.'

'Have you been hurt?'

'No. Getting arrested is the problem.'

'For what?'

'Assault.'

'Oh. Have they given you a record?'

'My special needs make me impervious to legal proceedings.'

'I was arrested myself a few months ago.'

'For fighting?'

'I was masturbating outside the Topaz in Tivoli. My psychotherapist thinks I'm scared of the city, that I got in trouble on purpose so that I didn't have to go there anymore.'

Jimmy shook his head gravely. He dropped his peeler into the bucket and stood up in his stooped way, indicating to follow him out the back of the kitchen. Stepping into the cold-punch of November, I found him proudly holding his bicycle for me to examine. It was a red and white racer, not an especially special kind, but fastened along various points on its frame were more of the thin sheets of metal from which his helmet was fashioned, contoured to fit as a kind of armour. On the front between handlebars and wheel was a shield, spray-painted black and white and emblazoned with a bike rearing up like a dragon.

'This is Destrier,' he told me, stroking the saddle affectionately while his head lolled and he stared into the middle distance. 'The shield is decorated with my colours and coat of arms. I fabricated it in the sheet-metal fabrication room in Duncree Training Centre. I painted it in the art room in Duncree Training Centre.'

'Why would you put armour on your bike?'

'Because now I'm not afraid when I ride out on it.'

'But it's just a bike with pieces of...'

'You tried to fight a city by masturbating outside a filling station. Thank you.'

That afternoon I watched him speed out of the hospital grounds, stood high on his pedals, his body stretched to all of its six feet. The sun cut through the cloud that had threatened rain all morning and set his helmet and bits of armour alight like a disco-ball. My mother died that weekend. She'd been dying for years but this time she died. She was to be buried in St Finbarr's cemetery in Glasheen, in the plot next to her mother and father with a place on the other side of her for my father and me when we got tired of not dying too. I wanted to go to the funeral so Susan helped me plan, breaking the day into steps. She prescribed extra medication for that morning, to take the edge off. I shit in my pants as my Uncle Phil was driving out the hospital gates. I told him what had happened and he took me back and that was the end of that.

‘I don’t know what my father will think of me doing something like that,’ I told Jimmy over the potatoes. ‘What do your parents think of you? What do they make of Destrier?’

‘I have to hide her from them now. Garda Sergeant Owen Farrell recommended she be dismantled.’

‘Where do you hide her?’

‘My friend Bryan from Duncree Training Centre has two mothers. I hide Destrier in his second mother’s garage. I cycle Rouncey most days, my other steed, but if I’m going to the city I take Destrier.’

‘Maybe sometime you could bring both and we could head out for a spin.’ I had my own prized bike when I was younger, an orange and yellow BMX. I can still picture that time and place, the memory of it unclaimed by the fog.

‘We could ride out together,’ Jimmy said, his lips parting into the barest outline of a smile, the first I’d seen on him. ‘You can take Rouncey. She’s small but she’s brave.’

‘Ride out where?’

‘The characteristics of a healthy adjustment to illness are optimism, extroversion, self-efficacy and an internal sense of control. We ride for the city.’

‘I can’t.’

‘We’ll see. I’ll come on Saturday, at nine.’

The rest of the week I fought with the idea, terrified by it, but I was at the main entrance to meet him on Saturday morning when he arrived with a bike on either side. He’d toned down the armour, insisting that travelling for war might encourage war. Rouncey was an ill-tempered racer that was at least twenty years old but the cables were new and she was oiled and reliable. We rode south, down into Glanmire and out the other side along a river that blew misty kisses into the air as it rolled toward the harbour. He set a pace that I struggled with and I began to panic, thinking he’d lead me back to Tivoli, past the filling station. Instead he stopped and we walked the bikes over the grassy mound to the harbour’s edge to examine the docks. He produced a pair of binoculars from his bag and examined the harbour.

‘All quiet,’ he said, handing them to me. ‘At least that’s what it seems.’

I peered across the water, tracing the Marina Walkway, where my father used to take me fishing when I was younger, back when it was greener, before they built the tunnel under the river. Jimmy leaned in conspiratorially, his eyes fixed on the grass at our feet. 'I say we take it by force next Saturday. Thank you.'

'Not this way. I can't go through Tivoli.'

'Then we don't go through Tivoli. We go up into Mayfield and down Summer Hill North. It's even better. No-one will expect it, like Hannibal going over the Pyrenees.'

'I can't, Jimmy. Not after what happened the day of my mother's funeral.'

'We'll ride to your mother's grave. We'll break through the lines and you can say your goodbyes. They can't take that from you. We'll arm you to the teeth.'

'I don't know.'

But he wasn't listening anymore. He was too caught up in the idea. We travelled back to the hospital in silence. I couldn't promise him anything. The wires that made promises had been severed forever somewhere in my head.

'I'm not going to be in work this week,' he told me as I handed him back Rouncey. 'I'm in Kerry with my cousin who is difficult and I dislike. My parents are gone to the Canary Islands for five nights. They don't take me with them anymore for various reasons. Meet me here the same again, nine on Saturday. I'll bring everything.'

He turned and began the journey to Bryan's second mother's garage, a steed on either side. Back in the hospital Dan quizzed me about what I'd been doing.

'Obviously there's nothing to prevent you from coming and going,' he told me in his slow, south-of-the-city drawl. 'We just need to know which Garda station we're gonna be picking you up from this time.' He laughed and slapped me on the shoulder.

The following week passed as slowly or as quickly as it always did. I was glad to have enough potatoes to peel but without Jimmy I was alone again amongst the clutch of chefs who laughed at jokes that didn't make sense to me anymore. On Saturday I awoke to grey skies and a heavy fog curled around the hospital so I put on the rain-wear my parents bought for me. Dan stopped me in the corridor and I told him I was headed for Mayfield to have a look at the city. It was easier for my brain to tell half-truths instead of whole lies. Jimmy appeared at exactly nine, the great-helm on his head, his elbows and knees protected by pads he'd spray-painted silver. Rouncey and Destrier were made up for the city this time. The wheels were encased in sheet metal so that nothing could get at the spokes. Fastened along the top-tube of each and extending out some five feet in front were lengths of painted wood. Destrier's lance was black and red, Jimmy's colours. Rouncey's was blue and white. He'd painted her shield the same colours and stencilled the number 21 onto it.

'My colours and coat of arms?' I asked.

'Yes.'

'Why 21?'

'It was the only stencil I had.'

'This is why you're called the Jouster?'

'This is why I'm called the Jouster. Thank you.'

I took Rouncey from him and he reached into his backpack and produced a silver cycling helmet for me, the same silver elbow and knee-guards that he was wearing and a wooden sword that he'd spray-painted gold. It was secured to a belt that I tied around my waist and he flicked his eyes at me to measure me up, nodding his wobbling head approvingly. We rode out, huffing and puffing against the climb as cars slowed and their occupants gawked at us. I felt like Jimmy and me were the only sane people left in the world. Everyone else had left home unarmed. We didn't stop until we reached the library in Mayfield, the peak of the climb. After he'd ensured that our armour would hold, Jimmy leapt onto Destrier's saddle and hurtled toward Dillon's Cross.

'Ride as if you've already beaten them,' he shouted.

I began to pedal, my heart crashing into the walls of my chest as I reached the traffic lights and turned left toward St Luke's and Summer Hill North. My nerve held as I descended but only because the hill made the decision, as simple as peeling potatoes. Stopping up at the river, I couldn't see Jimmy. The fear came, the sweat running like fork-lightning from beneath my helmet. I took it off and sucked ragged half-lungs of cold air from a world that had soured like old milk. There were three teenagers ambling toward me, two of them pointing and laughing, the other reaching for his phone.

'Poor fucker's still trying to get home after Halloween,' one said and they began to pick through my belongings, examining the lance and fabricated armour.

'Some skills for a handicap. Where'd you escape from?'

Warm salty tears mixed with warm salty sweat, blinding me. I pulled the sword from my belt, hoping that it might frighten them away but one of them pulled it from my hands. I tightened my shoulders, tucking my head down to protect me from my own weapon turned against me. There was an almighty thud that I presumed was wood on my scalp but when I opened my eyes Destrier was strewn on the footpath, her back wheel clicking as it spun. Beyond her, Jimmy was picking himself up from where he'd landed, examining the damage to his armour. The teenager who'd taken my sword was in a heap beside him, struggling to catch his breath.

'Ribs,' he wheezed and I reckoned he'd broken a few.

The others rounded on Jimmy who stretched to his full height, no lolling neck or sunken shoulders anymore. He drew his sword and slammed it onto the nearest head. The last of the three held his hands in the air like white flag and scuttled out of range.

'Get your sword,' Jimmy told me. 'They'll send Garda Sergeant Owen Farrell after us for this one. We need to get out of here.'

I did as I was told. Jimmy picked up Destrier and checked that she was ok, slashing his sword through the air menacingly in case anyone got ideas. The crowd that had collected to watch parted in front of us. Some of them recognised him.

'Up to your tricks again,' a scrawny fellow with a lame eye said, recording us on his phone like Jimmy was a kind of celebrity.

We remounted. Crossing the river, Jimmy began to make a kind of feral noise that I realised was his laughter.

'We've broken through,' he howled as we sped down Merchant's Quay and onto Patrick's Street. 'The city's ours.'

We stripped the armour from our bikes by the side of the old tax offices and Jimmy packed it into his knapsack, leaving the two lances by the kerb.

'It's all about stealth from here,' he told me.

'What if we meet them again?'

'Hide the sword down the back of your raincoat. Thank you.'

We pedalled on, deep into the south of the city where I'd grown up. The cemetery was peaceful, full of gentle noises, the wind chimes and the low creak of winter-striped, twisted trees. Jimmy waited outside. I took flowers from bouquets on different graves and I brought this little collection of uneven colour to my mother's freshly covered plot, next to her own mother where she'd had me lay flowers as a child. There was a picture of her beneath the newly-carved headstone. I stared at it for the longest time, trying to find a way around the damage in my head, to where I could feel what I was supposed to feel, but it was all gone in the fog. I put the flowers next to the photograph and pretended to say prayers I didn't remember. Then Jimmy and I began the journey back.

Poems by Jan Harris

Eva, Homo sapiens ssp. brokenheart

A notice on her compound reads – 'May bite – please do not feed' –
although she drew her teeth in protest at the trade in ivory.
She carved a tusker's name on each and wears them round her neck.

She's tucked behind the tapirs and sloths, but from the viewing deck
you'll see her fingers swarm to tend the ghosts of bears, lost
when the polar ice caps warmed. All she sees are shadows since her eyes
drowned in the floods. They've stuck electrodes to her chest, its rise
and fall as rapid as the squeak of pipistrelles. Her heart stopped
when the last Sumatran Tiger died. The shock waves felled trees

across the zoo. At half past five, when all the viewers leave,
she sings in voices of the past – po'ouli's secret chit chit chit, the
quagga's plaintive bray, the thylacine's whine and yip yip yip.

They're kind to her. She has a chair, a bed, a diet of soaps and crime.
They've matched her with a mate, a specimen from Seoul.
He's in his prime.

You, somewhere, among all this

Winter branches frame the overcast sky,
a canvas for distant birds,
featureless as blown leaves.
We watched them swoop together,
make ribbons, knots, bowl across grey
like aeroplane wheels on a runway.
Then we knew they were starlings, remembered
their sharp beaks, purple sheen in the sun.

Landing window, black sky –
a canvas for stars,
identical points of light
mapped on your bedroom wall.
You could point to Vega, Sirius, Rigel,
so familiar in their names
as we stared into the past, wondered
at their mysteries, their true nature.

You are travelling, travelling alone.
I imagine the pale disc of your face
sweeping through the miles.
See how those women glance
and murmur. The man at your shoulder
has a pool of words, a smile to dive into.
You gave me your trust. I am holding it tight
I will not let it go tonight.

~~

Kairos

the barn owl alights on felled pine
her slight weight on sturdy bough
heart face dipped in sunset

we gaze through thorn, speech frozen in our mouths
as if words might betray the curvature of her wings
the magnitude of her silence

She sculls light
rises to quarter the ground for mouse and shrew
while we turn for home, tugged by the same moon,
clumsy in her presence

Pathways, Walsingham Abbey

In place of barefooted pilgrims
children run on soles that flash,
ping gravel from paths like shooting stars.
Adults plead for a slower pace,
linger in shade where hoverflies hum,
    wing-beats blurred to human eyes.

Grass marks a passage of light between ruined walls
where cabbage whites tack like sailboats, reflecting sun.
Oak boughs nudge sycamores,
ancient trees, silent and still at the core,
yet even the smallest leaf lends voice to the wind.
        Prayers of centuries rustle here.

The east window stands alone now,
a reminder of skilled hands, rough with age;
others, young and clumsy, eager to master
the delicate traceries now lost to time.
The great arch, twin turrets point to sky,
    moon, Milky Way, galaxies beyond.

Jan Harris

The Protagonists

Kieran Lambe

There's nothing as wonderful on this Earth as routine. Routine is the sound of Vaughan Williams's *The Lark Ascending* at 6am, it's the hum of the kettle, the run of the shower, it's the creak creak creak of the floorboards underfoot, the sight of an outfit hanging on the back of the door, the dry taste of Weetabix with banana sliced in, it's the sound my home alarm makes when I type in the code, and it's the sound my door makes when I slam it shut behind me on my way out to work.

What's work? Work for me is the saying of things like 'I see on my screen here that you have not yet upgraded to our Premium Package would you like to…' and for the person on the other end of the line it's the saying of things like 'I'm not the one in charge of that decision. Goodbye.'

At 13:30 every day (Monday-Friday) I leave my desk, stopping only to smooth any creases in my skirt or to fix my hair, head downstairs, out the building and across the road to the Malone Café. I order a cucumber sandwich with dill and goat's cheese. To drink I have tea as well as a glass of tap water.

Fiona is nearly always the one who serves me. I'm thankful when she does because it means I can catch a glimpse at her dark cropped hair and the mole on her cheek. When we talk I say things like 'I'll have a cucumber sandwich with dill and goat's cheese. To drink I'll have tea as well as a glass of tap water please. Thank you,' and she says things like 'That'll be four pounds forty-nine,' and when she does she touches the side of her neck and I can see her nails painted purple or orange or somesuch other colour depending on the day of the week or some other code I can't crack, and I hand her a twenty pound note and when I do so I say 'Thank you,' and I think that is not the thing to say.

When I sit eating my sandwich and drinking my tea and my water, I look out the window at nothing in particular and think of nothing in particular except for perhaps how grey and cold the city can be. When I leave I try to catch Fiona's eye but in my experience she's always busy serving another customer. I'm back at my desk for 14:15 and by 14:30 I'm saying things like 'I see on my screen here that you have not yet upgraded to our Premium Package would you like to…'

On Tuesdays after work I go to the cinema on the Dublin Road because it's Crazy Tuesday and on Crazy Tuesday all tickets are three pounds. I usually see something with subtitles because there are fewer people in the audience and because seeing movies in French reminds me of Maebh – not because she was French (French people are seldom named in such a way) – but because Maebh was in the habit of bursting into French, saying things like *coup de foudre* or *plus ça change*.

I get salted popcorn (small) and a Sprite (medium). I used to get a bag of Minstrels too but I find that the crunching sound they make is distracting. The one behind the counter is, more often than not, a young lad with long hair that droops down over his eyes. His name tag says "Ciarán". He often gives me the wrong change; I'm in the habit of checking the coins after he hands them to me.

I sit in the same seat every time. Middle row, second seat from the right so that I can look at the screen from a slight angle. If I look at it straight on it all seems too big. When the film is done I stay until all the credits have scrolled off the screen and into God-knows-where. I gather my bag and my coat. I leave the theatre. As I leave I often see the cinema workers with black rubbish bags in their hands and they roll their eyes as I pass. I don't think you're supposed to stay to the end of the credits.

When I come home I usually see the man next door pulling into the driveway. His name is Philip and his wife is living with another man and he drives a silver Suzuki Swift (Philip, that is). He is in the habit of saying things like 'We're so in sync!' or 'Same time again tomorrow?' He has now put me in the habit of stopping at the garage on the way home to buy a pack of Polo mints or a bar of Dairy Milk even if I have no need for them.

At nights I usually cook pasta or chicken or an M&S microwave dinner. I watch the BBC News channel until ten and then I brush my teeth, climb into bed and spread out over the cold white sheet and sleep.

This has been the way of things since Maebh.

It's a Tuesday. Alarm, Vaughan Williams, kettle, shower, creak creak creak, Weetabix, work.

I go to the Malone Café for lunch. Fiona's there and I feel good.

'The usual?' she says.

'I…yes. How did you know?' I say.

'You work in the big building, yeah? You're usually here around half one. Still want the usual or are we changing everything today?'

‘Just the usual I suppose. One thing at a ti–’

And then she falls to the floor. People are running around and screaming things. Are they screaming at me? No. They’re saying things like ‘Call 999!’ and ‘Jesus. Fuck. Fiona. Jesus. Fuck. Shit,’ and I’m just standing there with a twenty pound note between my fingers.

It’s I-don’t-know-how-long later and the paramedics are here and they’re saying things like ‘Brain aneurysm,’ and ‘she’s dead,’ and ‘there’s nothing we could have done and that’s what happens sometimes. *C’est la vie.*’

I’m in the cinema now because it’s Tuesday and because it’s Crazy Tuesday all tickets are three pounds. I used to come to the cinema with Maebh, you see. When it was coming on Christmas we would go for a dander through the continental market beforehand, where there are stalls upon stalls selling food and flowers and trinkets. Everything smells of beer and bratwurst that time of year. One time I had a go at ordering some paella en español from the Spanish stall to impress Maebh. She had her French so why shouldn’t I have a bit of Spanish?

‘*Me pones una ración pequeña, por favor,*’ I said in a way so lovely and lispy you’d think I was Valencia born and raised.

‘Love, I’m from Lurgan,’ said the man as he scooped rice from the paellera and dumped it into a plastic container. ‘One fork or two?’

Later, when Maebh and I were walking to the cinema on the Dublin Road – that’s where I am now, like I said – we were finishing off the paella and Maebh says, ‘Well, I did love the sound of you speaking Spanish.’

On we went past the Pizza Express and past the Wetherspoons where a fat man with a red face was standing with a pint half-finished in his hand and a fag in his mouth and he said, ‘What’s the craic, ladies?’ On we walked to the Movie House. We saw a movie called *Midnight in Paris* which stars Owen Wilson and Marion Cotillard, who was wearing a flapper dress and her hair was finger-waved and she had on this lace headband that was black and beautiful and had feathers on it.

‘She looks like you,’ Maebh said and gave me a little kiss on the cheek and there was Marion Cotillard up on the big screen with her sad, dark eyes nearly closed and the screen was tinged like sepia and everything looked like an old photo or a page from a faded magazine. I wanted to cut it out and use it as a bookmark, or put it in the corner of the cabinet mirror in our bathroom at home. And every time I’d open up the cabinet to get my tablets or to check my makeup I’d catch a glimpse of it in the corner of my eye and think of my favourite place in the world, which is the Dublin Road cinema, and my favourite person in the world, who is Maebh and who is gone, and us sitting there in the middle row in the two seats on the end with nothing between us but a bucket of salted popcorn.

And here I am now on a Tuesday with an empty seat to my right and on the screen is Marion Cotillard only this time she's in a movie called *The Immigrant* and she's Polish and she's the protagonist and we're in New York and I'm thinking what about all those other people waiting in the queues at Ellis Island in 1921? All those little kids and the men and the women with tags around their necks. Aren't they just the protagonists of some other story that's happening off-screen?

And what about the boy whose voice hums – I can see him texting his girl during his smoke break, smiling when his phone lights up, or my neighbour Philip – I can see him now eating spaghetti and hoping his wife will come back through the door and say 'It's ok, it's ok, it's ok,' – or Fiona, who woke up every day and every day was just like every other day and then...And then Maebh…

And when the movie's finished I'm just sitting there watching the names of the director and the producers and the cast and the best boy grip and the set designer and they're all just scrolling up and away to God-knows-where and I'm just sitting there and there are tears.

Carolyn Lightens Up

by Barbara Lee

Carolyn was standing by her open window one evening to cool down during a hot flush, when her feet left the ground, her body tilted until it was horizontal and she began to float slowly out of the window.

'Argh! No! What the hell…?'

She grabbed at the window frame but it eluded her grasp and she made slow, steady progress over the back garden. She made some instinctive breaststroke movements to guide her until she found herself level with the enormous chestnut tree in the garden next door but one. She clutched a substantial branch and hauled herself up, where she sat breathing deeply and holding on to the branch until her knuckles turned white.

'OK,' she said aloud. 'I'm not drunk, I'm not mad and I'm not on drugs. Therefore I can fly.'

She sat in the tree for a few minutes until her heart rate slowed to normal, then she pushed herself off the branch and glided back to her open window.

Indoors, she wedged her feet under the windowsill to keep herself stable and pushed the window shut. Then she floated across the room and hovered above her bed until she gradually felt her body grow heavy again and sank slowly down onto the duvet.

Carolyn hated her downstairs neighbour. In his twenties, James was a floppy-haired golden boy with a well-paid job in finance and an air of privilege, as though good luck and success were his by right. He had a girlfriend called Camilla who did not live with him, but who was there every weekend and often during the week. She was small and blonde with a frequent high-pitched giggle which Carolyn guessed had once been called infectious, and she had been infecting people with it ever since.

In the summer they would lie scantily dressed in the back garden, James with his hand casually resting on Camilla's breast or thigh. Carolyn considered herself too old and too fat to lie around scantily dressed, her skin was too fair for sunbathing and she had not been touched by a man in years. She would watch them from her window and feel a murderous rage that anybody could be so young, beautiful and carefree. I'm going mad, she thought. I've got to get a grip.

Sometimes, in the evenings, she would hear James playing music, its thumping beat rising up through her floorboards. If she was on the early shift the next morning (and somehow these episodes always happened when she was) she would go downstairs and ask him, as politely as she could, to turn it down and he, equally politely, would agree to do so, but with a smirk which said, oh well, better humour the old bat. Upstairs again, Carolyn would realise he had turned the music down ever so slightly, but not enough to give her the peace she needed. She would curse him and reach for her earplugs.

Her next flight came three days after her first. She was just leaving her flat when she felt a sudden lightness all through her body. She grabbed the newel post at the top of the stairs and clung on as her feet left the ground and her legs floated out behind her. Then, to her horror, she heard James's door close downstairs. She saw him emerge from his flat. He stopped by the shelf in the hall to check the mail. Don't look round, Carolyn silently begged him. Please don't look round.

She held her breath while James sorted through the envelopes, pulled out two and slipped them into his jacket pocket. Then he opened the front door and went out.

Carolyn's sigh of relief was so great she let go of the newel post and began to float towards the front of the house. She flailed her arms to try to find something to hold on to but all she could reach was the smooth paintwork of the wall.

Her mind began to race. Somebody had obviously left for work already because the mail has been picked up off the doormat, she thought. Most likely Ben and Sharon in the ground floor front. The flat next to hers was empty. Mark on top worked nights and was probably asleep. Good. No one would see her. She let herself drift to the front door, grabbed the frame, turned round like a swimmer and was about to launch herself for the journey back to her flat when James's door opened again.

Camilla emerged, looking nauseatingly cute in a baggy t-shirt with a picture of a kitten on it and her hair sticking up at strange angles.

'Hi,' she said, rubbing her eyes. 'I thought I heard a noise and James had come back for something.'

'Oh no,' Carolyn said cheerily. 'It's only me.'

Camilla turned round and began to go back inside. Carolyn was about to launch herself again when Camilla turned round.

'Er... Carolyn, what are you doing?'

'Oh, I'm just looking for something.'

Camilla closed the door behind her. Carolyn glanced at her watch. She was going to be late if she didn't come down to earth soon. She looked through the glass panel in the door. It was a dark, rainy morning. No one would be looking upwards… yes, she would do it.

She reached down, turned the door handle and cautiously peered outside. There was no one about. Hooking her shoulder bag diagonally across her body she slipped out. It was an effort to close the door but she managed it by sticking one foot into the letterbox and pulling with all her strength, while holding on to the wall on either side.

Then a sudden gust of wind took her up into the sky. She screamed as her body was taken up above the houses and tossed and turned by the wind like a plastic bottle in a rough sea. She began to do the breaststroke to give herself some control. She looked down. Where the hell was she? A red bus, like a child's toy, made its way slowly down the road among other traffic. She calculated that it must be going in the direction of the station, and followed it.

Once her panic wore off she began to enjoy the sensation of flying. Her hair was blowing backwards and the wind and rain on her face, though cold, were exhilarating. When the wind changed direction and was behind her she found herself speeding up, all worries forgotten. It was more exciting than any of the fairground rides she had enjoyed as a child.

So caught up was she in her weightless pleasure she forgot to keep an eye on the ground and, with a jolt of panic, realised she was over the river, way past her destination. Turning round, she could see the sprawling buildings of the hospital where she worked. She circled her arms and drifted towards it and then, when she was directly above the flat roof of the Chichester Wing, consulted her watch. She still had plenty of time and turned on her back to await her descent with her arms folded across her chest.

When she regained her weight she dragged herself through the trapdoor on the roof. Pam, one of the other nurses, came out of a side ward, saw Carolyn and raised her eyebrows.

'Have you been on the roof?'

Carolyn realised from her encounter with Camilla that people will accept the most preposterous statements if you make them with conviction, so she smiled at Pam, said, 'Short cut,' and hurried to the cloakroom to repair the damage to her hair and face and change into her uniform.

Just after midday, when she was beginning to think about lunch, one of Carolyn's post-operative patients began to haemorrhage, much to the horror of her daughter who was visiting. Carolyn swung into action with her usual efficiency, bleeping the surgeon and alerting the blood bank before leading the patient's daughter, a timid mouse of a woman, into Sister's office for a calming cup of tea.

Carolyn sat opposite the woman and explained that haemorrhage sometimes happened in cases like her mother's and although it looked alarming, with prompt treatment was usually not a serious cause for concern. While she was in the middle of her explanation she felt the familiar feeling of lightness take over her body and she slowly rose out of her seat. Desperate, she decided to continue her explanation in the cool, calm voice she used on anxious relatives, her body still in a sitting position and bobbing gently just below the ceiling like a balloon on a string. The patient's daughter looked at her with huge eyes, a tissue pressed to her mouth, unable to say a word.

'So, if you'd like to stay here and finish your tea, I'll go and see how your mother is getting on.'

'W-will you come back?'

'Of course.'

Carolyn straightened out her body and swam to the door, ducked under the frame and hid out in the loo opposite until she sank to the ground.

She began to keep a diary of her flights. They all occurred either in the morning, when she was rushing to get ready for work, the middle of the day or at night during a hot flush. However, that was as predictable as they ever got. Sometimes she had three flights a day for two days, then none for a week.

Most of all she enjoyed her night flights; the sense of total freedom from care as she allowed herself to be carried on the breeze, the power she felt as she used her arms and legs to control her direction. She loved, too, the naughty sense of voyeurism as she glided past other people's windows, feeling sorry for the tired-looking woman who stood at her ironing board while her pig-like husband swigged beer in front of the television, and laughing delightedly at the two handsome young men who, clad only in their underwear, engaged in a vigorous pillow fight. One night as she swooped past a window her heart nearly stopped as she found herself looking directly into the face of an old man, but then added her sigh of relief to the rushing air around her as she realised it was the blind man at number 26.

Her morning flights were riskier. It was winter, and the wind carried her to the hospital at a brisk speed. Below her, pedestrians kept their eyes to the ground or straight ahead, but what would happen when summer came?

She managed to keep her noon flights a secret by arranging to take her lunch break at the time she knew she might take off and heading for a deserted ward in the old part of the hospital where she would swoop and soar, all thoughts of illness and pain forgotten, until she felt heaviness return to her limbs. Then she would go to the hospital library where she would read everything she could find about the menopause, but could discover no instances in the medical journals of menopausal women who could fly.

Spring came, and Carolyn solved the problem of how to avoid being seen in flight by changing to the night shift. This meant she was at home for her morning and noon flights, gently floating around her bedroom with her eyes closed.

At night she would simply allow herself to float above the beds of her sleeping patients, propelling herself up and down the ward with front crawl movements of her arms. What she would do if one of them awoke and needed attention she did not know.

At home, however, the problem of James and Camilla continued. Although she was out of the house when they played music at night, a spell of warm weather meant they spent their weekends out in the garden, listening to music on the radio, accompanied by Camilla's infectious giggle. On two occasions, she leaned out of the window (it was a time of day when she did not fly) and asked them to turn it down, explaining that she was working nights and needed to sleep. They obliged, but not without exchanging looks of irritation. The third occasion was on a weekday, both of them having taken the day off work.

Angrily, Carolyn stuck her head out of the window.

'Damn it, I've told you I'm working nights. For Christ's sake turn that racket down and stop being so bloody selfish.'

This time, James sneered at her and said, 'Shut up you boring old bitch. We're entitled to listen to music if we want to.'

Camilla chimed in, 'Why don't you move out if you don't like it?'

Before she could think of a reply, Carolyn felt the familiar sensation of her feet leaving the ground and her legs floating behind her. She drifted out of the window, aware of James and Camilla's faces, blank and open-mouthed, below her. It's the wrong time, she thought. I never fly in the afternoons. Then, she felt heavy again, not gradually as before, but all at once, and came crashing down to earth, to land on James. Camilla stared at her, then ran squealing indoors.

She never saw Camilla again, and there were no other witnesses to the incident as all the neighbours were at work. Carolyn, her fall broken by James's body, was unhurt apart from a few bruises. She struggled to her feet, returned to her flat and went to bed, where she slept until it was time to get up for work. James's body was found by Ben, who lived on the ground floor. A policeman questioned all who lived in the house.

'I'm a nurse, working nights,' Carolyn told him. 'I must have been asleep when it happened. Honestly, officer, I had such a tough shift last night I don't think anything could have woken me.'

The policeman, a veteran of many night shifts himself, sympathised. Carolyn heard no more about James and as far as she knew, his death remained just another unsolved mystery.

After that, Carolyn never flew again. Mostly she was relieved, but occasionally, when she stood at her window at night, she would watch the top branches of the trees swaying in the breeze and long to be up there again, enjoying the sensation of being carried far above the trivial concerns of everyday life.

Home Movies

by Bruce Harris

The best days of your life is what Uncle Malcolm keeps on calling school days when he talks to me, or rather at me. I think he means I should be enjoying every cosmic minute of mine, because he did his. As Uncle Malcolm is loaded enough to paper the walls, you can't help thinking his schooldays really must have been something else, Bermuda Dream Academy, maybe, with a lagoon for a school pool and kids hula hooping around the school gates. The trouble is, he always describes his school as a grim Victorian pile in the north where anything even faintly naughty would cause you to be beaten to a pulp. Maybe Uncle Malcolm is a closet masochist, whose seven holidays a year are all a front.

I discovered the word "masochist" from my brother and he, believe me, would know. He's still at university, and seriously into athletics; he says it has the "potential for glory", but I think it's mostly about stopping himself from spending money. At the end of the lawn, there's a wood and iron thing which Mum calls a summerhouse and we call the Park Bog, and on a daily basis, Sam's in there "training", panting away on treadmills and dumb bells. He keeps saying to me, you ought to be doing this, Mark, keep you fit for A level crunch time next year. The guy's insane. I tell him, listen, bro, you should know as well as I do that you don't need to be fit to do exam courses, you just need to be able to sit listening to people for hours until your bum numbs and your will to live drains away. Nothing whatever to do with muscles, pecs or PBs. Sam's always on about PBs. I thought at first it was some weird sexual position (Pelvis Bending?) until he said it meant Personal Best. 'You should always', he says, when he forgets that he's my brother, not my dad, 'seek to improve on your Personal Best, whatever you're doing'.

It's a hot August day – it happens – and I've got all sorts of other stuff to do. I'm still catching up on A level year 1, and after that I'm supposed to be preparing for A level year 2, and since I didn't prepare properly for year 1, I know only too well what will happen if I don't prepare for year 2 – I'll be even further up what's-it creek with even less of a paddle. I've been up in my room with the window wide open, trying to improve my PB on getting through the day without being bored out of my skull. Revising, it's called. Unfortunately, I'm at the stage where if I don't do a *Great Escape* out of this work dungeon for at least an hour or so, I may well go completely insane, which won't get me through the exams either.

So, in the name of escapism, or something, I'm going to take my current smart gadget home-movieing round the garden and record for posterity, whatever that is, what my barking family are up to, so when I resume being bored witless in classrooms, I can do *My Summer Holidays* for my fellow inmates, the lucky people. I am usually invisible, it seems, to my siblings and parents, which is all to the good for these purposes. And if all else fails, it'll get me a grade in Media Studies.

So our family documentary, our *Redfern Times*, begins behind the Park Bog. Sam's in there, bare-chested; for a terrified moment I think he's naked. I've got nothing against Sam's nakedness apart from chronic feelings of inadequacy and despair. But no, shorts are on, though he looks warm enough to make me thankful that I'm not "training". 'It's not just for running races, you know, keeping fit, Mark,' he says to me, with that eye-roll thing he does when he means sex. He's got a girl friend called Maddy, and that's a good name for her, because she spends her entire life obsessing over some detail of her face which she thinks isn't beautiful enough or something. I reckon she'd do best to find a mask which looks like what she wants to look like, clag it on and save herself the bother.

Finding Sam and Maddy "at it", to use Uncle Malcolm's phrase, really would be champion news footage. Apart from private viewings at school, I could blackmail Sam with it for the rest of eternity, particularly as I happen to know that Maddy's Ma and Pa think Sam and Maddy are keeping themselves "chaste" before marriage. Maddy's chased all right, down to the place near the riverbank where they don't know I know they go. I've caught glimpses of what happens when he catches her, and I'm pretty sure it's not what Mr and Mrs Maddy have in mind. Trouble is, the chances of Maddy being in there while Sam is working out are pretty much nil really, because Sam sweating like a horse is not, frankly, at his romantic best. Moving on down the side of the lawn, through those trees with hard green apples too sour to eat so you wonder why anyone bothers, I can see Maddy in person. True to form, she's with my sister Kate – she probably spends more time here with Kate than she does with Sam. They're about the same age, nineteen or so, don't press me.

They can't see me behind this tree, but they wouldn't notice if they could. They are both lying, stark naked apart from little bits of cloth top and bottom, in the full sun, in that kind of gob-smacked torpor which they get into on days like this. It's either TOWIE or melanoma go for it time. They're both smooth and entirely hairless. If they ever find as much as one tiny hair anywhere, they start putting great strips of Elastoplast stuff all over it to tear it off while they screech a bit. Our attitudes to hair are a bit different; for me, the more the merrier, each new arrival meaning I'm moving further away from spending the rest of my life with the physique and sexual magnetism of Pinocchio. They think, like – help me, or within three months I'll be all over YouTube as the – like – sensational Bearded Lady.

I don't linger around with this, partly because there's nothing happening except the occasional sigh and turning over to give the back a go, but mainly because I should not be getting a bonk on looking at my brother's Intended. That's what my mother calls Maddy. Sam's Intended. You can hear the capital letter, as if she's trying to convince herself. I wonder sometimes how much it would be worth to Sam for me not to pass on the news that he's probably moved on from Intending, but the trouble is, of course, that it might be worth me not getting his boot in my backside. I think briefly about stripping down to my Marks and Sparks slip ons and going right over there to join them. Free country. But maybe not. Apart from getting burnt to a crisp unless you smear yourself in that slime stuff, even worse than having a bonk on looking at your brother's Intended is said Intended seeing you have a bonk on looking at her, meaning being grassed up to both parents as a newly discovered Pervert.

I move carefully on to the group collected on the lawn, consisting of my dear father and mother, alongside Maddy's folks. They're all gathered round a wooden table which my Dad sometimes makes out to be a Family Heirloom, though I know for a fact that he got it three years ago at a second hand furniture shop. It's distressed, he says, and I'm not surprised, standing out in all weathers having drinks chucked all over it and Duke the labrador peeing up its legs.

I'm moving carefully here because if my mother sees me, it's going to be, 'Mark, darling, come and join us,' followed by the aside to Mrs Maddy – 'he's absolutely slogging away with A levels, but all work and no play, really.' Then it'll be sit there and keep schtum until we think of whatever it is we've left in the house, then it's 'would you, Mark darling,' and I'm off to the house without knowing where the sauce/wine cooler/mayonnaise/bottle-opener is any more than they do, meaning trailing back to them like a prat for my mother to tut loudly and say 'if you want a job doing…' etc. And, all the time, Dad will be eyeing me with that 'why aren't you working?' look. And even if they don't need errands, there isn't a chair because they're on all four of them so I'll be sat on the ground with lawn damp slowly soaking my pants and several hundred garden insects dropping down my neck. And I'll have to Socialise.

My mother calls Socialising, 'conversation, dear, social niceties, communicating politely with people.' I call it Putting It On.

Take my dad, for example, with Mr Maddy, alias Mr Metcalfe, Christian name Don.

Now I happen to know Dad thinks Don Metcalfe is something of a thickie, to be honest. 'Philistine through and through,' I've heard him say. 'Culturally vapid. The kind of man who thinks Handel's *Largo* is a light ale.' Yes, I know. Family joke. Yet here he is, grinning away at Don and occasionally even nudging him. 'Beer on the lawn, Don old man. Not often the opportunity arises, in this pestilential climate of ours.' Don is looking like he always does, along the lines of how our English teacher Harry Phipps describes people who give him stupid if well-meaning answers, "amiably vacuous". Eyes engaged, just nobody home. A few beers have obviously already gone down the hatch, because Dad is even looking at Don with a grimace of something like friendship, instead of slyly peering at the man when he thinks no-one can see him as if Don had just dropped out of the drainpipe.

Mum is also, at the moment, all over Mrs Metcalfe, Doreen, like a rash. Doreen is spread over her chair like a landed Zeppelin, an acre or so of buttock exuding on either side. How a woman of her size can be related to slimline Maddy, I don't understand. Maybe Doreen was set up to have quadruplets and Maddy was the only one who managed to get out.

By carefully weaving in and out of patio plants, barbecue ovens and patio heaters, which Kate sits toasting herself next to when Socialising demands sitting out in autumn, I reach the safety of the trees and shrubs in the garden bottom left; 'a taste of environmental wilderness in the managed garden,' says my mother, which basically means no-one can be bothered to trim it down. Here lies my soul mate Duke, with the good sense to just take it easy while occasionally breaking off for a little leisurely butterfly-chasing. Duke is the only creature in this place who always exhibits pleasure when he sees me, and he is up, tail wagging, before I'm within ten feet of him.

I realise how hot I am as soon as I've moved out of the direct sun, so I take off my top, one of my bluest and coolest, which even Alison Shaw looked at me in for almost five seconds, and hang it on a branch. I realise that if I don't think of something to do very soon I will either have to return to "revising" or also remove my cool blue jeans for the purpose of stringing myself up on a strong branch with them and ending it all. The first is boring and the second a little embarrassing; I'm not sure I want to be found hanging with nothing on but a pair of M&S slip-ons, however acute the despair may be. One or two compulsive death jerks might even mean my last action in this world would be to flash my bare bum at it, so something else – anything else – is probably a better idea. I decide on a little movie of old Duke, just for a change. He suddenly looks as if he's coming over all star struck on me, tail going berserk and tongue lolling about, and I'm having a therapeutic giggle when a substantial clod of earth hits me right on the upper arm, only just missing my nearby bluest and coolest top by a short neck. For a few seconds, I'm wondering when labradors acquired the ability to chuck dirt around, but then a definitely non-canine cackle from the branches above puts me in immediate contact with my sweet little brother Philip. And a more high-pitched cackle suggests little Barry Metcalfe is up there as well.

We've done units on care for the environment and our fellow species in Geography and Biology, and there's stuff about how all the creatures on the planet have a value and a right to be there, and I can only think that whoever put the courses together had never met my brother Philip. He's now aged 13 – Sam 21, Kate 19, Me 17, Phil 13. We were talking about it once and concluded either that Mother and Father had stopped taking proper precautions or Mum had had some kind of broody afterthought. Our birthdays are all suspiciously close together round March and April, and my folks habitually take a holiday in June or early July, 'before the hordes, dear, and the heat.' One final rogue night after wine and summer moonlight and little Phil is the ghastly consequence, a kid totally devoted to pesthood who is only ever really happy when someone in his vicinity is spattered with something or jumping up and down in rage. 'Psychology of the youngest, trying to get attention,' Kate says, and having been there for a while before he came along and being still invisible a lot of the time, I can see where he might be coming from, which makes it all the more irritating when he starts on me. In this case, my brotherly protests get as far as 'Phil, if I have to come up there–' before another spatter of something unspeakable hits me right on the neck and not far off the eye. I reckon that could only have been little Barry. Now being spattered by your own flesh and blood is bad enough; being spattered by a mini-Metcalfe is quite another. But, mad as I am, I hang back from setting off on an errand I'll probably regret, since the pair of them can climb trees like little chimps. Something more subtle is called for. I note one or two points and direct my gadget at their grinning faces.

‘So – trip to Brighton beach next Saturday, little boys wanting to go, aren’t they?

I’m right on Phil’s chirpy features, now not quite so chirpy.

‘I wonder what your mummies and daddies are going to make of my home movie, lads. Little Phillie’s high up a tree, one of the ones Daddy’s particularly told him not to climb, hasn’t he? Little Phillie’s in his best shoes, the ones Mummy’s very forcefully told him not to wear for things like climbing trees, hasn’t she? And what’s that I can see just peeping out of Barry’s pocket? A good strong catapult, I think, isn’t it, Barry? I remember hearing what Barry’s Daddy thinks of Barry’s catapults before. I think perhaps he won’t be too pleased. What do you think, Barry?’

Now they are both gratifyingly silent and I can see Phil’s eyes going all pleady.

‘You wouldn’t grass us up, Mark, would you?’

I take the phone away, feeling a pang of something, sad git that I am.

‘No, probably not. Just don’t pelt me with crap, brother, and don’t let your little pal do it either. I came here to talk to someone sensible.’

I sit down next to Duke and let the little boys scatter off to be pests somewhere else.

‘You know, Duke,’ I say, and he’s all ears – well, and tongue, and tail. ‘The truth of it is, that if him and me could swap, and I could go back to messing about in trees and chucking mud at people, playing at monster alien mutants with pockets full of chewies and plastic dog mess and catapults–’

A shriek from the other side of the lawn as Maddy suddenly leaps to her feet indicates clearly enough where one plastic spider/dog mess has just been in action.

‘…I suppose I probably would. As it is, I’m going to have to do all these expletive deleted exams and in a few years’ time, I’ll probably finish up in the shed with Sam, sweating buckets and working on my PBs. And according to Uncle Malcolm, the best days of my life will already be over. Human life, Duke. Human life is a total mystery.’

And they say dogs don’t nod.

Poems by Mark A Murphy

Innocent Blood

Whose innocent blood is this?
Where did you see the innocent blood?
Was it the innocent blood of a child, a son or daughter?
Was it the innocent blood of a mother or father?

Who found the innocent blood?

Was the innocent blood spilled in al-Byada,
in Gaza, in Bengasi, in Odessa?
Was the innocent blood spilled in your land?
Was the innocent blood spilled in the morning or the evening?

Did you declare the innocent blood innocent?

Was the spilling of innocent blood a massacre, a holocaust?
Who is guilty of innocent blood shedding?
Why was the innocent blood shed under heaven's gaze?
What is to be done with the innocent blood?

Did you mop the innocent blood?
Did you cross your self and pray at the sight of the innocent blood?
Did you leave the innocent blood abandoned in the street?
Did you bury the innocent blood?

Whose innocent blood is this?

The Garden

What can the thrush know
of Epicurus
as it takes another worm from under the rose-bush
though it is composed of the same atoms as us?
She speaks no language
we humans understand
and certainly reads no ancient Greek
though we consider her singing voice beautiful.
What use her suffering to us?
There is no god
of thrushes that can help her
bring home the bacon
or understand the nature of reality.
The proof of quarks
in neutrons and protons
is of no use to the thrush
who builds her nest of twigs and straw,
while godless man hypothesizes
about warp drive engines propelling him to Alfa Centauri
in under two Earth weeks.
On the garden gate the thrush swallows the worm,
we are not sure
of what she is thinking or if she is capable
of rudimentary thought
but she sings her songs, as if for us, throughout lunch.
Absorbed, we meditate out back
on the Epicurean epitaph:
I was not; I was; I am not; I do not care
as we digest the atoms in our greens,
happy to be alive.

Mark A Murphy

Voodoo

by Alison Wassell

The little fabric doll lies forlornly on the charity shop shelf, having seemingly been cast out of the toy box by a horde of half-naked Barbie dolls. She is flat and unbendy and her badly embroidered face is set in a pinched, disapproving expression. Mark, who has brought me shopping in an attempt to cheer me up, is momentarily distracted from his search for Star Wars memorabilia to sell on eBay. He picks up the doll and waves it in my face.

'Who does this remind you of?' he says. I see what he's getting at instantly.

'Eileen George.' Even the name of our boss makes me feel ill. Mark says he's going to buy the doll for me.

'You can stick pins in it next time she has a go at you,' he laughs. The lady on the till charges him 10p, and says that actually she'd happily pay him to take the doll away. It gives her the creeps.

At home, I prop the doll up on the mantelpiece. As I sit with my laptop balanced on my knee, attempting to plan next week's lessons, she seems to be watching me. I get up and turn her face to the wall, then go to the kitchen and pour myself a glass of wine. I was never much of a drinker, until Eileen George came into my life.

On Monday morning I scuttle into school fifteen minutes before the children, having spent the last few hours dealing with a plumbing emergency at Dad's house. Eileen George silently looks at her watch and frowns. She informs me that she will be observing my first lesson. I know she's supposed to give me more notice than this. As always, I nod submissively and say nothing. I rush to my classroom and throw books and equipment onto tables as my heart pounds. With two minutes to go before the bell I realise that I have left my USB stick, which contains all my planning, on the kitchen table with my packed lunch.

With a shaking biro I cobble together some kind of lesson plan, knowing as I write that it's a lost cause. Eileen George has hated me since the day she set eyes on me. The bell rings and I go to the classroom door to welcome my class. Ryan's mum waves his reading book irately in front of my face.

'This book's too easy for him. You need to move him up a level,' she states. She's wrong, but I don't argue. What do I know? The children swarm into the classroom. The wind is howling, which always makes them more wild than usual. They shove and bicker over the coat pegs. Amelia begins to howl more loudly than the wind. Someone has kicked her. A bruise is already beginning to blossom on her frail white shin. I search in vain for the culprit. My classroom assistant has failed to materialize.

Finally, the children assemble on the carpet for registration. Amelia is still whimpering. Eileen George makes her entrance, complete with clipboard. Grim faced, she sits on a child-sized chair in the corner. One of the children raises a hand.

'Mrs George is here,' he says, clearly being of the opinion that I am too stupid to have noticed. I smile my brightest smile.

'Mrs George has come to see how clever you all are,' I say. Eileen doesn't even bother to acknowledge this. She writes something down.

The children seem unusually fidgety. I ask if anyone can remember what we learned last week, about adjectives. Not a single hand is raised. Ryan fiddles with the Velcro fastenings of his shoes. Amelia wipes her nose on her sleeve and turns to whisper to her best friend Kylie, who is attempting to plait her hair. Rebecca, with one thumb in her mouth, twists her other hand inside the gusset of her knickers. Eileen scribbles on her clipboard again.

'An adjective is a word that describes something,' I remind the children. Sophie raises her hand.

'Need a wee,' she declares.

Somehow, I stumble my way through my introduction to today's work, and prepare to send the children away to their activities. Bradley Tucker has been unnervingly quiet. He chooses this moment to erupt. Before I have had time to write up today's learning objectives on the interactive whiteboard he has upended a table, sending books, pencils, crayons, chairs and children flying to all four corners of the classroom. Eileen George rises, stony-faced, to her feet.

'I think I have seen enough for today,' she says. She looks at me over the top of her glasses and tells me that we need to have a serious talk.

I know from experience that the serious talk will not happen today, or tomorrow. Eileen George will leave me waiting in fear and dread for weeks on end. Then, one day when I have actually begun to hope that the whole episode has been forgotten, she will pounce. On my way home from work I stop off at the Co-op and buy a bottle of red wine.

Two glasses in, I remember the doll on the mantelpiece. I take her down and stare into her ugly puckered face. She seems to be judging me. I stumble to the drawer that contains my sewing box and take out my sharpest needle. I stab her in the eyes, several times. It makes me feel a little better. She remains poker-faced. I go to bed, leaving tomorrow's planning undone.

In the morning I take the bus to work, fearing that I may still be over the limit. Arriving only twenty minutes before the children, I anticipate Eileen George's disapproving gaze. She is not there. She appears to take morning assembly wearing dark glasses.

'What's up with the boss?' I ask the secretary, at morning break.

'Conjunctivitis,' she says. Apparently, she's never seen such a bad case. Not that Eileen will go and see a doctor. Doctors are for weaklings. When her mother died she took half a day off for the funeral. She is the one person in the world who will die wishing she'd spent more time in work.

Eileen stays in her office for most of the day. I almost relax. Even Bradley Tucker seems bearable, despite the fact that, several times, he uses me as target practice for his blu-tack missiles. Sophie finally gets the hang of tens and units. I remember why I am a teacher.

I travel home on an emotional high, and, for the first time in ages, don't even bother to stop off to purchase alcohol. While I'm eating my healthy jacket potato and salad in front of the TV, the Eileen doll catches my eye. Something seems to have happened to her face, and she now appears more afraid than disapproving. I get up to examine her more closely, and conclude that some of her embroidered features have simply come undone. I feel strangely benevolent towards her.

'No torture for you tonight, Pet,' I reassure her. I put her away in the drawer with my sewing kit.

Eileen's conjunctivitis continues to trouble her for the rest of the week. She leaves me alone. I begin an art project with my class. We create our own version of the Sergeant Pepper album cover. It covers a whole display board. As we work, we listen to Beatles songs. We sing along to *Yellow Submarine*. Bradley Tucker smiles at me, for the first time ever, as he peels dried PVA glue from his fingers.

At morning break on Friday my phone buzzes as I am making a cup of tea. It is my Dad's neighbour. Dad has had a bad fall and is on his way to A and E. I gather up my things and prepare to leave, stopping at the office to explain. Eileen emerges from her room and physically bars my exit route.

'Surely there is someone else who can see to him,' she says, although she knows that there isn't. I stare at her until she moves out of my way.

‘We need to have that talk,’ she calls, as I hurry away.

I arrive home in the early hours of Saturday morning, after Dad has been admitted to a ward. When I switch on my phone I find a message from Eileen, informing me that she has referred my unauthorized absence to the governors. In the back of a cupboard I find the whisky I reserve for colds and flu. I pour myself a large glass, then remove the doll, and the pins, from the drawer.

The weekend passes in a blur; full of hospital visits, despair at Dad’s seeming inability to face life on his own, half-baked lesson plans, late-night drinking sessions and the occasional tormenting of the Eileen doll. Not by nature a violent person, I am not particularly vicious in my pin-sticking. I do little more than tickle mini Eileen with my sharp object, hardly piercing her pathetic cloth body.

I arrive at school on Monday morning fully prepared to defend myself. In the early hours of the morning I have composed a speech about how some things are more important than work, and about how I was brought up to put family first. I intend to throw in a couple of digs about how not everyone shares these values. I will, after all, be talking to someone who once left her sick teenage daughter waiting at the walk-in centre with a broken ankle and proceeded to school as though nothing was wrong. I smile to myself, walking up the path from the car park, as I anticipate the battle to come.

For the first time ever, Eileen George is absent. I raise an enquiring eyebrow at the secretary. She leans confidentially towards me, raising her hand to her mouth to shield her words from some inquisitive Year 6 pupils who have come to collect the registers.

‘A rash,’ she whispers. An all over the body kind of rash. She winces as she speaks. Eileen fears it could be scabies. I somehow resist the temptation to giggle.

I spend the day in a kind of euphoria, free from the dread that Eileen will appear unannounced in my classroom like one of the Dementors in *Harry Potter*, sucking the joy and life out of everything. It begins to snow, and I abandon literacy hour to take my class outside to catch snowflakes.

Monday is staff meeting day. At 3.30 Eileen appears in the staff room, visibly uncomfortable and fidgeting in her chair. Nobody elects to occupy the seats on either side of her in the circle. As the meeting progresses we all begin to itch and scratch.

As the meeting draws to a close, Eileen announces that she will be absent for a few days, due to unforeseen circumstances. She is vigorously rubbing her arm as she speaks. Feeling elated at the prospect of the carefree days ahead I make for the door. She stops me in my tracks, putting her whole scabby body between me and my escape route.

'We need to meet,' she states. She will be coming into school after 3.30 on Wednesday, once all the children have left. I smile.

'Looking forward to it,' I say, flippantly, certain that she has lost her ability to hurt me. I anticipate the damage I will do this evening to the Eileen on my mantelpiece.

I give Mark a lift home, the weather being too bad for his usual cycle ride. He wonders why I am not more concerned about having been summoned.

'Remember that ugly little doll you bought me?' I say. I tell him the whole story. The conjunctivitis, then the scabies. Once is a coincidence, but no way would it happen twice, unless I had some kind of power. Tonight, I tell him, I'm planning to gouge out Eileen's heart with my needlework scissors.

I have known Mark since our PGCE days. He looks at me as though seeing me for the first time.

'You have seriously lost the plot,' he says. He is so disturbed that he forgets to remove his bike from the boot of my car when I drop him outside his house. He tells me I need to cut back on the alcohol, especially on school nights. I smile, and wave cheerily as I drive away.

I am more concerned than I care to admit by his reaction, though. As I wait for my ready-meal to heat in the microwave I stare at the Eileen doll. She stares back as best she can with the few features she has left. Suddenly appalled at the desperate, delusional person I have become, I consign her to a supermarket carrier bag and take her out to the wheelie bin. I also empty half a bottle of wine down the sink. I eat my ready-meal without tasting it, and go to visit Dad in hospital.

In the morning I phone in sick. I huddle under a duvet on the sofa, listlessly channel hopping between *Homes Under The Hammer* and Jeremy Kyle. On a normal day Jeremy cheers me up, because my life is marginally better than those of his guests. Today I fear I am destined to become one of them, in my cheap leggings and oversized t-shirt. I open up my laptop and Google "jobs for failed teachers". I complete an online questionnaire that assures me I am suited to a job in financial services. I go back to bed.

In the evening, when I go to visit Dad, he tells me, for the thousandth time since Mum died, that he needs me to give up work to look after him. For this first time ever, this seems like an enticing prospect. I take Wednesday off too, although I present myself at school by 3.30 for my scheduled meeting with Eileen. By now, I have given up, embarrassed by the fact that I allowed myself to believe, even for five minutes, that I have any kind of control over what is to happen to me, and what I laughingly call my career.

My letter of resignation is in my handbag. With some kind of perverted pleasure I look forward to the moment I toss it onto Eileen's desk and tell her to stick her job where the sun doesn't shine. As I get out of my car Bradley Tucker, on his way home, hurls himself at me like a missile. He throws his arms around my waist and presses his face into my jumper.

'I've missed you,' he says. I briefly allow myself to run my hand over his Velcro-like hair.

'I've missed you too,' I tell him, before stumbling into school.

Eileen George has compiled a dossier on me. Her eyes flicker with glee in her blotchy face as she turns the pages. There is a record of the time I abandoned my class, for two minutes, to free a bird that was trapped in the cloakroom. Every parental complaint is there, every time I failed to hand in my planning on time, every box I failed to tick, every piece of meaningless homework I failed to mark. She goes on and on. It has long since grown dark outside. The caretaker taps on the office door, begging for permission to go home. Eileen assures him that she is perfectly capable of locking up the school herself. The two of us are left alone.

Finally, Eileen closes her document and looks up at me. She is tugging at her collar, as though she is uncomfortably hot, although the heating has been turned off. Beads of perspiration mottle her forehead. Her hands shake slightly, and from time to time she clutches at her left arm. Her eyes twinkle, though, when she says the words 'Capability Procedure'. Every teacher knows that this signals the beginning of a slow, painful death to their career.

Time is running out for me to jump before being pushed. I rummage in my handbag for my letter of resignation. Before I can place it on the desk, Eileen rises to her feet, making a weird sound as she struggles to breathe in. She staggers towards the door, clutching at her chest, and collapses before she gets there. Her skirt rides up far enough for me to see her enormous knickers, and a ladder in her flesh-coloured tights. Her eyes plead with me. My hand closes over the phone in my pocket.

I take it out and gaze at it for several minutes. Eileen ceases to struggle for breath, and an eerie silence descends. I crouch over her, and feel for a pulse. There is nothing. Her eyes are glassy and unseeing. Saliva dribbles from her mouth. I wonder if I could unpick her features, like those of her poor cloth lookalike. I don't bother to try. I pick up my handbag, step over her corpse and leave, humming a tune to myself as I go.

'*Ding dong, the Wicked Witch is dead…*'

Cappuccino Time

by Cedric Fox-Kirk

Today is New Year's Day and it's raining. It seems to the older of my minds, being able to look back over the years yet to come, to have been raining in England forever. To the younger of my minds, well, it's just too confused to think about it – it's having trouble coming to terms with being absorbed by its older self. This "older self", the one in Cyprus infusing elderly bones and muscles with the Mediterranean sunshine, is the one that really knows what's going on. It's the one that knows (has known for decades) that I am about to embark on the single most stupid course of action in my entire life… to date, that is.

It was the early sixties; I mean it is the early sixties: Kennedy has been assassinated and the Beatles and the Stones are taking over rock and roll. I'm in Nottingham at seven o'clock on a wet and windy night crossing the street to meet Janice. Garish street lights illuminate the scene. This is my vision of her, the wet street, and the harsh lights with Janice standing waiting for me at the centre, which has monopolised my dreams for the last fifty years. She will be nineteen this year so it has to be New Year's Day 1964. And that means the trick has worked: I am in the right place at the right time and in the right mind.

'Hello, Janice.' I make my voice sound relaxed, like nothing's wrong. Maybe I'm letting my younger self do the talking but I'm certainly doing the thinking.

'Hello, Ronnie,' she answers. Coming closer she rests her hand on my arm and looks up in the expectation of a kiss. God, she looks lovely: I can't let my younger self deny the reality of this but, no need to worry, my younger self is dumbstruck. He has just realised he can foresee the future. Reality is in flux and I am in play!

In the life already lived I told her it was over; in blunt, boorish syllables that came from some young teenager who knew no better – and was sick from not really wanting to. At the New Year's Eve party – I'd gone without Janice, who was at a family "do" – I got drunk and bowed to the constant nagging from the gang to 'give up that bird' and 'stick wi' yer mates, Ronnie'. In the sixties they didn't use the phrase "peer pressure" but that's what it amounted to so, even though I loved her kind nature with that sassy streak flashing through it, I had been browbeaten into ending it.

But now I am about to transform reality. I lean forward and give her the expected kiss. She responds and the kiss of greeting acquires passion. She snuggles closer, saying 'it's a cold wind – where shall we go, Ronnie?'

I look at her, a fresh view through young eyes, while my stupefied younger self cannot take in what is happening and fades further into the back of my mind. I reply, 'New Year's Day, not many places open – but the new coffee bar over by the Tech College is. Can we go there? I want to talk, got lots to say to you.' Catching her look – a fading smile, a questioning glance – I quickly add, 'nothing to worry about, but I've got a story I just want to tell you, and to maybe have a chat about us.' I throw in a broad smile for good measure and Janice smiles back. I keep telling myself – older to younger – to keep it cool and keep it steady and this should work like a dream. Wrapped together, we cross Parliament Street and walk towards the new Tech College building. Janice is right, it is cold – with thinning clouds running before a brisk breeze.

Pubs open on New Year's Day and so does this particular coffee bar. It's pretty busy when we get there but we order our cappuccinos and claim the table in a little alcove in the corner. Janice slides into her seat – an advantage of being slim – and tucks her long legs, unkindly called skinny by my mates, underneath the table. She opens her coat: a tight-fitting pink jumper shows off her curves. I've always loved the way she does that; for a slim girl she has surprisingly well-rounded breasts. It all makes the older self realize just what a dimwit this earlier version of him was – is! No slip ups, boy! She looks at me, one classy bird: dark hair, long dark eyelashes and round cheeks dimpling with a smile just for me.

In the older self's past, the younger self walked away from this gorgeous girl and was, at this point, in the pub with the gang trying to erase with alcohol the feeling of having made the most monumentally idiotic mistake of his life. But reality has changed.

Decades from now and two thousand miles away I came across the means to tap into the brain's timeline, the mindline as I hear it called.

Everybody has a mindline; science hasn't described it yet but it's the thing that fixes your memories in place as thoughts move forward through time. It naturally has blocks that shift in concert with time. I met people who were already practising reality change on their own lives. I cajoled or blackmailed them into teaching me the trick. It worked, I discovered I was one of a tiny percentage of the human race who could mentally circumvent those blocks and send my mind back down the mindline. I have done it… and I have changed my world. There may be a reckoning at some point in the future. I know it but I can handle it.

In the new now, I tell her, 'My mates said I should finish with you but I don't want to.' I watch her expression go from pleasure to alarm to relief in a flash and I know that notwithstanding all the risks lurking in the immediate future, what I am doing will be worth it. So I continue 'Janice, I have no intention of losing you; staying with you may well be my only chance of having a decent life. I mean it.' God I want this to work, to persuade her there is something special between us. The fact I mean every word gives it a credibility I couldn't manufacture.

'Oh! Ronnie, why would you want to split up? Anyway, it sounds as if the idea came from those useless mates of yours. Ignoring them makes you seem so much more mature.' She reaches for my hand, still looking into my eyes and says, 'I really… like you.' My hope is that the slight hesitation means she is thinking "love" not just "like", but "more mature" seems an odd phrase to use and sounds a faint alarm. I must proceed with caution.

The waitress arrives with our cappuccinos, then I take a deep breath and plunge on. 'I have this story I want to tell you. I've thought about telling you for… well, for a little while.'

Just two months we've been going out together so I'm careful to avoid saying anything Janice might find weird. No way will I tell her I've loved her for fifty years and that my idiocy in breaking up with her has haunted me through an unfulfilled life – marriage, divorce, a son and daughter who ended up closer to their stepfather than me, grandchildren I don't know, an aimless middle-age – culminating in throwing over all my ties in England to try and do something with myself in Cyprus. At least, I had thought, I can be miserable in the sunshine. But it was there, near the village of Pissouri, that I was drawn to a small coterie of people in the ex-pat community who led quiet, unassuming but seemingly well-fulfilled lives. And there I stumbled across the great secret that, for a very lucky few, there is a way to change the world.

Now I am using that knowledge and I need to build upon the change I have just wrought: I need to consolidate. Indeed, even as I planned this takeover of my past self and prevented the split with Janice, It struck me that illustrating the emptiness of what could have been my future life was the best way to convince her I was her man – for the rest of time.

'An old man sat down one day,' I tell her, 'to reappraise all that had happened in an unhappy life and asked the question we all ask from time to time – if I could change just one event in my life to make it a better one, which would I change? And the old man went through all his life from childhood through schooldays, wishing he'd worked harder, had different friends. He considered his youth and things he could have changed then, his marriage and all the steps in it leading to an inevitable divorce. He considered the emptiness of his lengthening years and the last gamble of moving abroad to find something to give a final purpose to his existence. As he surveyed the drab landscape of his history one event stood out, one event that said 'just change this and you will change the world' and that happened on New Year's Day 1964 when he broke up with his girlfriend.'

Janice has listened intently to every word of the tale and says, 'What a sad story. It's meant to be you, isn't it? So what happens next?' It seems an odd question and, at the back of my mind warning signals are flashing on. However I decide to press on

'Ok, Janice, let's assume this is the future, indeed let's assume it's my future then let's assume what happens to the old man is this…'

'There is a collection of villas in Cyprus,' I tell her, 'all occupied by people, mostly Brits, who are so different from your average ex-pats ... and so different from anyone else I have ever known in the world. The old man – ok, I'll say "I" – I came across them by accident, just traveling around, and realised I had stumbled across some really special people. I watched them, became absorbed in the careful way they kept themselves apart, never had visitors and all had the most disconcerting way of circumventing problems; they had perfect lives. This old man we are calling "I" realised this didn't happen naturally, not for people living in a small community off the beaten track in Cyprus. There had to be a trick that maintained it, particularly as, watching them, I noticed they changed from day to day in subtle ways: A man with a walking stick suddenly had no need of it, walked as if he never had needed it, a woman I saw in tears one day was bright as a button the next, as if she'd never been anything but cheerful all her life.

Finally, I got it. These people had the ability to change their past, not to affect the present of any disinterested parties but only their own and those close enough. It must mean a bit of juggling to iron our inconsistencies and adverse effects but they seem to manage it, easy if you lead a quiet, remote existence. The strange thing was I didn't find it unbelievable … because I wanted it! I was determined to confront them with my discovery of their secret and I was a complete stranger and had never intruded in their past lives. And today it worked.'

'But it's not really a story with an ending, Janice, just my way of saying that if you and I broke up with each other it could have...' the realization comes that "telling it like it is" was not the good idea I thought it would be, so it is time to forget it. So I just finish, 'I'm so glad I haven't been that stupid.'

'You are saying that if you had been stupid enough to split with me, when you get old you'd want to find a way to come back and change it all – but that's impossible, of course.' She sips her coffee, gazing at me with a thoughtful expression that doesn't fit the words, 'or is it? You tell me Ronnie. You're a boy of eighteen, very likeable but no Alan Sillitoe. I can't believe you dreamed up such a fantastic tale just so you can persuade me you don't want us to split up. All you had to do was…was… just carry on the way we were. This is way too clever for you to come up with.'

My only thought is damage limitation. Quickly, I say, 'Janice, I could have done something that would have hurt us both and my story is meant to show you what my life would…er, could be like without you.'

The Janice who replies sounds like an older, self-assured woman, 'Come on, Ronnie, no eighteen-year old can think like that – Unless I'm to believe this weird fantasy about some commune in Cyprus inhabited by time travelers, that's all pie in the sky. Let me carry on your story, let me assume this amazing tale is real: how did you do it, Ronnie: what trick did you use?'

'No tricks, Janice. It's just a story.' I'm frightened; this isn't the way it should go. Both my body and brain are tightening up. The girl I'm talking to shouldn't be saying these things.

'No, Ronnie, not a trick but using the mindline. I bet you found out that the brain's timeline acts as a conduit, transferring thoughts to memories as it goes from past to present to future – a conduit with a one-way valve keeping pace with time. But help me here, let's say you found out about this and let's say you found out that a few people could mentally open the valve and take over the thoughts of their past self at any point they chose. Then your story has an interesting development.'

'Yes, yes, very clever of you to carry it on like that.'

'Not clever, just lucky. I mean lucky in that of these few people who can turn off the valve, there are some who can sense changes happening that affect them, and can move their minds back till they find the point where the change is happening.'

I am dumbstruck and can think of nothing to say.

'You see, Ronnie, my life after you dumped me got better and better. I met the right people, married a good guy, traveled the word, wrote articles and books and indulged a passion for oriental art and history. I became fulfilled. I thought a lot about you, you were my first love but,' in one fluid moment she is on her feet, still speaking: 'no way am I having some geriatric second-chancer take away my life and rearrange it to suit himself.'
As she walks away she looks back and says, 'Your cappuccino's gone cold.'

The Artist and his Model

by Harvey Martin

I always dress up before leaving now. He says it saves time and he's always ready to start when I arrive.

Last week I dressed as a homeless person. He gives me the clothes on a Friday and he likes me to try them on at the weekend to enter into the part. I wore an old khaki parka, black fingerless gloves, torn jeans and dirty plimsolls without socks, and absolutely no make up.

From Boston Manor to Green Park I tried to look lost and depressed. During the journey I was given three pound coins and a cup of black coffee, and a very nervous young man told me that Jesus loved me.

This week I'm playing a tart or, as he calls it, a woman of the night. I'm wearing a curly blonde wig. My face is heavily made up, with bright red lipstick on my pouting lips. I have a tight white blouse emphasizing my cleavage, fishnet stockings and four-inch heels. My short black fake fur coat is on the seat next to me. It gets so hot on the trains. I notice there's a few men hot under the collar. I must be entering into the part. So far I have been given nothing: no pound coins or coffee, and no more messages from Jesus. Among the men sneaking a look at me is a large businessman who looks as though he would give me more than a few coins for my services. I hide my face and start to read the *Metro*.

I saw the ad in the *Evening Standard*; dangerously close to those ads for live sex chat. *Artist seeks Girl, willing to dress up and stay still for hours at a time.* I remember thinking, with an ad like that no one on this earth would call him; and I've been with him now for three months. Anyway, I needed the money.

I arrived at his studio at 9am and am now sitting cross-legged on an old bar stool. I'm trying to sit still. I'm bored, but trying to look seductive. He must be having trouble with my mouth. There is an awful lot of red-coated rags being thrown into his bin. He's certainly a serious painter. He hardly talks, and works hours without a break. He hasn't made a move on me yet … or asked me to strip off.

The blonde wig has slipped a little to the left; he doesn't seem to notice. I think he's back on the lips again, judging by his brushful of vermilion. He never lets me see the painting. At the ends of the sessions he always covers it with a light cloth, so I can't sneak a look on the way out. I sometimes think he rubs it out when I've left and starts again in the morning. In fact one day, close to the end, he seemed to be using a rag a lot more and rubbing quite vigorously. He could be an abstract expressionist, or maybe I'll look like those ugly women De Kooning painted.

Sometimes he caresses the canvas with his brush and hovers over it; the brush moving from left to right. He looks like a conductor with his baton; or he's like a surfer waiting for the perfect wave. The perfect move of the brush with just the right amount of colour. He often works quickly, as though caught in a frenzy; as though he's being led by the brush like some kind of magical wand; capturing a moment, leaving brush marks like a Frans Hals portrait. Oh, here comes the rag again. He can't seem to get the mouth right.

At the end of the day he told me that this would be the last time he would require my services. He thanked me and gave me an invitation card to the private viewing at the Thompson Gallery on Bruton Street, next Friday.

I found the gallery easily enough. I showed the girl my invitation, grabbed a glass of white wine and moved towards the first painting. It was a naked figure. I presumed he was sharing the space with another painter, artists often do that; but the face looked suspiciously like mine.

I glanced around. There were small groups of people chatting, one or two sitting and some gazing at the paintings. Every painting had a naked figure in a variety of poses. All their faces were my face. I felt a rage moving within me, rising up through my chest and about to explode from my mouth. People were looking at me. How could he be so deceitful?

I gulped a few mouthfuls of wine and tried to relax as I went back to the first painting. I knew the clothes that she should be wearing. It was the character of the athlete. I remembered the tight red shorts and the blue vest very well. I recalled his words to me, every day that week. 'You are about to run for gold at the Olympics. Concentrate, look straight ahead, let nothing disturb you, see the finishing tape.' He had captured it perfectly, not only my face, but the nakedness seemed to enhance the fragility and tension of the moment; about to explode forth from the blocks. The body wasn't mine, but one from a remarkable imagination.

Of course as I moved on through the exhibition, I knew the clothes the figures should be wearing by the emotions that showed on my face and the pose taken up.

Then I came to the Woman of the Night. Seated on the bar stool cross-legged and naked like the others. The wig was there, the heavy make up and the pouting lips. There was a tremendous vulnerability in this figure. As though she was extremely uncomfortable being observed. Just as I had felt on the train that week.

He had portrayed them all with compassion and tenderness. He seemed to have captured all the variety of emotions that led them or drove them on as human beings.

In the last painting a woman sat naked on a stone cold floor, somewhere on the underground. Her arms clasped her knees and drew them up, covering her nakedness. It was an astonishing portrait. There was such a sadness and fear in her face and yet such a longing for intimacy, as she gazed up watching the people pass by. There were three pound coins near her bare left foot, an empty cardboard coffee cup and one of those flyers you find on the tube. *Jesus loves you*, it said. Jesus loves you.

Poems by David Crann

Tea-bagged

Across the rims of tea-cups
tilted like quarterdecks
our eyes met like salvoes,
taking no prisoners.
The decks were littered
with morsels of the lifeless
whilst we capered
as sole survivors must.
The voyage is long.
The weather is ramshackle.
The sheets hum like albatross.
The prow heaves like tomorrow.
Wilderness is no more,
and the wild places
are safe harbour for us now.
Panic has waned
to a hazy star on the horizon.
And the horizon –
were it possible to reach it –
bids us home.
Afternoon tea has frozen us.
Ever the clock chimes four
like the minute-gun at sea.
Ever is the minute caught
in a noose of light
that tightens like a tourniquet
to bind our disparate selves
and save us from the night...
all this from a sipping of teas
of a May afternoon
to a forgotten song.
A prodigious music has been born
as eternal as we shall ever know.
The helmsman's wheel revolves
random through the stars,
the prow bent to chanced horizons.

The barque might seem rudderless
among a havoc of shooting-stars
but we are safe together,
the table-linen spotless,
the teapot smoking,
our lips burning, our eyes watering
across the rims of tea-cups
tilted like quarterdecks.

~~

The fish-market in Nice

The fish-market is ending. The vendors of fish,
their voices harsh against the screaming of the gulls
and dialects as indigestible as fishbone, toss snatches
of fish-flesh to the vacant hullabaloo of gulls.
These flap from far, and wide, and nearby vantage points –
roofs and posts, flagpoles and mastheads – crazy at the helm –
like a sea-flung plague, bright pebbles skimmed
across the quays by a sea-god's boy.
The English cannon roguishly resounds
to knell midday and blunt the battles on the quays.
And off the population marches au pas de gymnastique
towards aperitif, sole meunière and table wine. Above,
a van Gogh sky collaged in slabbed palettes of blue;
below, old-photo faded gulls plunge and lunge, with van Gogh
sunflower-yellow bills – bright daggers to impale the ephemeral titbit...
and skewer sibling rivals at the kill.
No time for recalcitrance or politesse: the diners,
all sharpened elbow, crack their wings to claim their place;
and forks, like beaks, stab down; and knives, unsheathed,
make nonsense of the etiquette of gulls.
Grace before meals? The gracelessness
of gluttons leaves the hungry starve.
Town-far, a ghostly cormorant detonates black water
and emerges, like Excalibur, with a brandishing of hope.

David Crann

Fried Eggs

by Colin Heffernan

SomTIN hz hapnd n # 19

That's all the text message from Tammy said. Worried, Dermot climbed onto his bed and squinted through the net curtains. Across from his house was Number 1, where she lived, but her sitting room and bedroom windows were turned golden unknowns by the bomb-blast of a late April sun beginning its evening dip. The only movement was the slow turn and jingle of the little set of wind chimes that hung outside the windowless skeleton of Number 3 next door, put there by Tammy in her efforts to decorate the estate. Her driveway was empty, her parents still at work. She was in the house alone with the stooped and time-scorched grandmother who had come to live with them last year, bringing to seven the population of Roundwood Estate in Watergrasshill.

Wt? he sent back and waited the long wait of an eleven-year-old boy hanging on the word of the thirteen-year-old girl he was in love with.

W8 til l8r. caL aftR dinr. parNts gone 2 cinema 2nt.

He moved the messages to the folder in which he kept everything she sent him, a precious digital map of where their two lives merged. The phone was worn out, a hand-me-down that his parents gave him for emergencies. Tammy teased him mercilessly about it. Her parents bought her a shiny smart-phone last Christmas that warbled and chirped with messages and updates. Sometimes she showed him the videos and images she received, the oddness that queued up on the Internet like cars in traffic. Other days she gave him the phone and turned director, pulling faces for him to photograph or posing in the new clothes that appeared after each fortnightly trip to the city with her mother. She sent these images to ping-pong across a world he was not allowed to be a part of. His phone didn't even have a camera. Instead it had a game called Snake that his father insisted had been a great hit years ago. He'd shown it to Tammy and she teased him all the more.

Accepting he'd have to wait to find out what was afoot, he turned his attention to his school-bag, agonising over what to do with his uneaten lunch. Usually he'd stash the sandwich under the set of bookshelves in his room and bury it in the kitchen bin after dinner when his parents separated to living room and upstairs office. Only last time he'd forgotten them there and he'd brought mice in. His father rigged every corner of the house with traps and spent a whole weekend stalking the outside walls with a silicon gun, cursing build quality, his greatest vexation. Riddled with guilt, Dermot cast the blueing, nibbled remains of those sandwiches through the un-windowed window of Number 32, praying he could draw them away from his father's murderous rampage. He'd eaten his lunch every day for four weeks as penance but the recession had taken a terrible toll on his sandwiches and the cheap ham and cheese and the horrible, doughy bread had ground him down again. He double-wrapped today's abomination in tissue paper and hid it behind the framed photograph of him meeting Liam Neeson who played Qui-Gon Jinn in the last Star Wars trilogy. He'd dump them in Number 32 later. That was where the mice would build their kingdom. He and Tammy had no use for it.

Downstairs his mother was cooking, the steam from a pot of boiling potatoes cocooning her behind the misted glass of the kitchen windows. She had her back to him, chopping at an onion with a merciless rhythm that set her shoulders to shaking like they did when she cried. He took his schoolbag to the living-room table and began his homework, the rote-learning of Irish rivers and mountains that they'd be expected to map on the whiteboard tomorrow morning for Mr Williams, the choices becoming narrower and more obscure with each turn like some kind of geographical Russian Roulette. The radio was turned to talk-time. Talk-time made his parents angry but they listened every day, nodding solemn though they surely knew it by heart. Tammy said her parents listened to it as well. They'd gotten on well at first, their families, but they'd fallen out over how Tammy's cousins parked their cars when they visited. It seemed strange to be getting cross over a couple of cars the same week that the estate's sewage system exploded. Tammy told him that they couldn't get along on account of her parents paying for his father's public service job. It made Dermot ill at ease, imagining Tammy's dad having that sort of power over his family. It made him wonder if it wasn't smarter to keep quiet about the bad parking. He might have said something about it only Tammy's father arrived home that same evening driving a different work van.

'Look at this prick,' his father barked, peering out the living-room window through the blinds. 'Moaning about money all along. I thought he couldn't afford to go halves on putting the gates up at the entrance.'

'Typical,' Dermot's mother agreed from where she'd snuck in beside him to catch a glimpse of the second-hand but pristine white van that was coasting to a stop at a spiteful angle half on and half off the little strip of tarmac between the two houses, The Mobile Mechanic writ large on back and sides. 'Bought with what he hid from the taxman no doubt.'

Dermot leaned across his spread of school books to look through those same blinds now but there was still no movement. He wondered what this latest adventure would involve. Number 19 was a nearly-finished house further along an estate in which only their two were lived in. The rest of it ran like a Lego manual in reverse, all the way to what would have been Number 42 at the end, its bricks still stacked on the palette that they'd been delivered on, everything slowly dissolving back into the ground. Tammy had spent the day at home from school pretending to be sick. She'd gone exploring. Her grandmother disapproved of almost everything but she liked to see children outside so she encouraged Tammy to get amongst the rusted edges and broken glass of the crumbling estate while her parents were working. It stung him, to think of her going out without him. She might have happened upon someone else. What scared him most was that someday the builders would come to put roofs on the piles of bricks and Roundwood would fill with older boys who were smarter and funnier and would take her away from him.

'Back to the homework, nosey,' his mother told him, folding her arms disapprovingly. 'She'll still be there later on.'

His father arrived home from the office at six, the tiredness hanging from him, pulling his skinny height down into a stoop. Watching him unload the day into the correct places, he looked to Dermot like someone retracing his steps, his brow furrowed, on the trail of something he'd lost. He ruffled Dermot's hair and kissed his wife in a preoccupied way and went upstairs to change. He would eat and go to his office, to the online world in which he seemed happier.

'Dinner's ready, Dermot, love,' his mother told him.

She began to bring plates to the table, her eyes red with onion-damage. Dermot's father re-appeared in his evening clothes and they sat to eat. Outside Dermot could hear Tammy's mother arriving home, her father following in the van shortly after. His own mother made a face, as if this reminder of their neighbours' existence had soured the taste of the food in her mouth. Not that it could get much worse. Everything she cooked was riddled with the anxiety that ran through her like an untraced leak, from the overcooked, browning broccoli to the shrunken, dehydrated chicken. Early on in this terminal culinary decline, Dermot's father laughed at the tiny fillet on the end of his fork and declared, 'Put these back in the oven for ten more minutes and we'll have diamonds to cover the mortgage.'

She didn't speak to him for two days. Still his parents nearly always brought smiles to the dinner table. Between mouthfuls of food his father liked to list the *Sold* signs he'd seen on the way home. His mother would nod eagerly and for a time it would seem like this was real, not the battered worksite in which they lived but rather an onrushing wave of opportunity that they held a prime slice of. Dermot knew they did this for him, to maintain the brittle pretence that his world was safe. They didn't understand that the possibility that things were getting better terrified him most of all. Of the downturn he understood this – so long as it was so, Tammy and he were together and it was just the two of them.

Dinner finished and dishes tidied away, he ploughed into what remained of his homework before shuttling it upstairs to the dimly lit office for his father to check. Dermot found him sat in front of a flickering screen that was filled with his latest writing, what he'd explained was a blog on sea fishing, his passion.

'You'd a good day in school?'

'Uh-huh. We learned about rocks.'

'What did ye learn about them?'

'Where they came from, that limestone used to be little animals and that's why water flows through it.'

'And what about the other types?'

'That it takes longer but eventually the water gets them too.'

'So all's fair in love and rocks?'

'I suppose.'

'Me too.'

'Can I go over to Tammy?'

'How are her parents when you're over there? Are they nice to you?'

'Uh-huh.'

'Good. Do they ever say anything about us?'

'No.'

His father nodded slowly. 'Ok, go play or whatever it is ye do but be careful. No mucking about.'

Tammy. This was what his day built to. The rest of his existence was spent mythologizing her, the soft pinkened lips and honeydew breath, the lithe, golden-skinned frame that seemed possessed of a different energy to his own, as if it burned with the blue flame of an efficient gas rather than the hissing, popping wet wood that propelled him at an uncertain angle and speed. And she'd begun to change in magical ways, growing out where she'd only grown up before. She had allowed him to touch the miraculous orbs that were emerging on her chest, just the once and only for a moment. She said her mother called them her fried eggs and that he was the only one she'd allowed put his hands on them. That made him happy, knowing that whatever else she shared with her friends on her phone, this was his privilege alone.

He cleaned and spruced himself, sprayed on the deodorant that she'd commented on once and he'd worn ever since. He sat at the window of his bedroom and waited with the lights turned off until her puppy-fat parents emerged from the house and climbed into her mother's battered silver MPV. He caught her father looking across at his house and he froze in the window, knowing from school that predators couldn't see you if you didn't move. Once they were gone he stuffed the sandwich in his pocket and he sprinted downstairs, assuming a careful, studied pace once he was outside in view. He waited next to her father's new work van, leaning against it with one leg propped on its bumper, striking the kind of relaxed pose he felt might impress her. She appeared, resplendent with her red-flavoured long hair and huge blue eyes made all the prettier by the worry that filled them.

'It's not good news,' she told him. 'I'm afraid things are going to have to be done.'

'Ok. I trust you.'

'Good.'

'Are you still sick?' he asked her as her grandmother spied a look at him through a slight parting of the curtains, her bespectacled little eyes running through him like swords.

'No. It was one of those eight-hour bugs.' She hauled open the back door of her father's van and dug out a torch. Next she fetched a shovel from the side of the house and handed it to him. 'You'll need this.'

'Why?'

She didn't answer. Beyond their houses, the un-surfaced road wound like a snake between the unfinished buildings. Here and there lay bricks and piping and wires, cement turned to meaningless sculptures by rain, the bags stripped from them by two harsh winters. Everywhere they planted a foot crunched snow-like with broken glass. Their parents had given up calling the Gardaí when they heard windows shattering in the night. They never came quick enough to catch anyone and rocks had been put through most of what yielded to rocks now anyway. The fencing that the Council erected to keep people out had been kicked down so that Tammy and Dermot were able to sidle through a gap and into that warzone, Dermot clutching the shovel close to him, hoping as he did on every adventure that he might find an intruder bent on harming them, a chance to prove himself to Tammy.

'What did you do for the day?' he asked, the anxiety still gnawing at him that she'd done it with someone else.

'Television,' she told him. 'Then I practised my violin and Nanny made me soup for lunch. I think it was the worst yet. After that I checked on the house.' The house was Number 19, their house. 'Anything happen in school?'

'No.'

'Nothing?'

'Rivers. Rocks. That was it.'

'Did you miss me?' He blushed and wrung his hands, the shovel tucked under his arm. 'I hope you missed me,' she decided.

They ambled down that dusty overgrown pathway, what would have been the estate's main thoroughfare, what should have been alive with other children and their trappings, with parents and such an abundance of cars that one or two parked awkwardly might never have mattered to anyone.

'You'll miss me even more next month,' she said as she sprang up and over the weed-pocked heaps of gravel that had been delivered to line Roundwood's driveways.

'Why?' he asked, scrambling after her in ungainly fashion.

'I'm off to the south of France. We're going to live in a tent for three weeks. Daddy surprised Mom with the news at dinner. I don't think she was happy. She says we'll be like tinkers.'

This was a new torment to occupy him. France would be full of French boys. At least the older boys in school were knowable. They had the same gangly failings as he did. Now there was France for the summer and then she was off to secondary school in the autumn. It was like a kind of waking nightmare.

'Ok. Is that the bad news?'

'Afraid not,' she said solemnly.

Number 19 was the strange love-child of whoever had half-built and then abandoned Roundwood. The roof was on and the doors had been put in. It was almost completed while the others around it were still incubating somewhere on a set of abandoned plans. He and Tammy had decided one weekend that this was the home they would make together. She had probably forgotten but the idea had solidified for him into a vow to finish it, brick by brick, window by window. Once it was done he would fix the breached fencing and seal them inside the crumpled nether-estate forever, just the two of them.

'I made it safe,' she told him, pointing at put-in windows that he saw were covered with cardboard. 'My cat would have made mincemeat of her.'

'Her?'

She stopped him at the door, planted hands on his shoulders and for the first time ever he saw tears welling in her eyes. 'I need you to do this thing for me. It makes me so sad and I can't...I just can't.'

'Ok,' he said, bewildered, frightened even.

She switched on the torch and pulled opened the plywood that had been erected over the front door, just enough to slip inside. He followed her and watched the beam of light in her hand search through the darkness like a coin chipping away at a scratch-card.

'I can't find her,' she told him. 'Take down the cardboard. She'll be safe with us here anyway.'

He did as he was told, skewering the house with sunlight. From the kitchen he heard Tammy calling him. He found her cradling a rabbit. 'I saw it earlier out the back. It's got myxomatosis. I looked it up on my phone.' The rabbit was breathing hard. Its eyes were swollen closed, red and puffy like his mother's from the onions and the talk-time radio. 'I didn't want the cat to kill it. That would have been an awful way to go.'

'Maybe we can fix it.'

She shook her head. 'We can't help her. The best we can do is to make it painless.' She handed it to him, careful with it. He felt its heart thumping against the palm of his hand, a fever-drum. 'You have to do it. I can't bear the thought of it.'

'Me? How?'

'I don't know how.'

'No way, Tammy. I can't.'

More tears escaped, twin droplets running the kamikaze trail of her lovely reddened cheeks. He felt trapped, as cornered as the rabbit would have been if the cat had found it.

'It'll be fine,' he said. 'It'll die in its own time. Or maybe it'll live. Who knows?'

'It'll suffer.' The tears ran over her lips and into her mouth. 'You have to. For me.' Knowing the power she held over him, she lowered her eyes and said, 'I'll let you touch them again if you do it.'

'That's not fair,' he pleaded.

But the rabbit's fate was sealed. She stroked the wretched, bloated little creature in his hands one last time and went outside. The rabbit hadn't moved since he'd taken it from her. It seemed barely conscious and yet life was pulsing from it, the body taking command, pushing its temperature skyward in one last hopeless charge against the disease that was killing it. To Dermot, that microscopic battle seemed neither his business nor the rabbits, as if they were both caught up in someone else's war. Still there was no escaping what needed doing. He took the rabbit's body in one hand, caught its head with the other and twisted sharply. He felt the snap and shudder of its death, the heart stuttering, denied the rhythm of the brain. He stood paralysed until all semblance of life had fled from it, exhaling the breath he'd held throughout only when he heard Tammy asking him if it was over. He brought it outside to her, outside to the fading evening. He dug it a hole next to Number 19, having dreamt of many things to plant there for the two of them but never this.

'Thank you,' she said when he'd buried it and smoothed the earth so that soon there would be no evidence of what he'd done for anyone to judge. 'You can touch them now. If you want to.'

'I'll do it tomorrow.' He could still feel the awful sensation of the rabbit's neck snapping. He needed to put some distance between him and that waning warmth in his hands so that he could properly explore this other unexpected warmth that had slammed into his world like an asteroid when Tammy first offered it. 'I should get back.'

She nodded and they closed the front door of their home and set off. She held his hand on the way and Roundwood Estate felt like his empire, simple as it was. Back inside Number 2 his parents were busy examining the sheets of numbers that his father printed off each month, the bottom-lines of domesticity. They asked what he and Tammy had gotten up to but he didn't tell them. Their secrets were their own. He mentioned the holiday in the south of France and his father's face clouded over and his mother rolled her eyes.

'They'll probably pitch the tent in the middle of the road,' his father said.

Dermot shrugged and slid hands into his pockets, discovering the tissue-wrapped sandwiches still there, little lives hinging on little mistakes.

Storm Light

by Jasmina Svenne

No time to hesitate. No time to think. The deceptive light still gleams upon the lime-plastered walls. But now it has turned yellow-green-grey. A rumble of thunder on the horizon, coming closer, closer.

Dear God, don't let it rain – not now the hay has been cut. Just two more days. Two days and the hay will be dry and we can stook and thatch it…

Every single window in the house standing open in a vain attempt to air it, so stifling has it been all day. But now a trickle of air is insinuating its way into the house, hinting at the storm to come. Pa nowhere in sight. Nobody else to do this but me.

One window shut, another. Up the stairs. Don't trip over the hem of your petticoat. Shift sticking to my skin. Stays squeezing hot air out of my lungs. Another window closed, another. Only one more, one more room. Hurry, hurry.

And then a voice.

'Martha.'

I whip round at the last window. Lightning flashes behind me. The room illuminated in the tiniest detail for an instant. A figure in the corner where no figure ought to be. A man in my bedchamber.

Sudden darkness. Vague shapes in the dimmed room. Another rumble. So close. But still no rain.

Silence save for the pounding of my heart, the sharp, pained rasp of my breath.

'Martha, it's me.'

A shape moves out of the shadows and I see him properly in the ghastly storm light, coatless, hatless, white shirtsleeves gleaming like snow.

'Seth?' I whisper.

It can't be true. My mind must be addled. The nights have been too short, too broken for sleep. Too much to worry about. Suppose the harvest fails this year too?

Or suppose this is a ghost. Ma Wetherell said it happened to her grandmother, that her husband appeared to her in her bedroom at the exact moment of his death, falling from his cart, drunk, coming home from market.

But the hand that grips my arm is real, strong, sinewy, dark hairs sprouting on the wrist. Callused fingers embedded with gunpowder, chafing my skin.

'Yes, Martha, yes,' he whispers, his face now so close that even in this strange light, I can see the dapple of blue-black along his jaw. 'I came back – for you.'

The wind is picking up. It rattles the window, like a wayfarer lost on the moor, begging to be let in.

'But – no – I don't understand. You – you went for a soldier. You –'

You left me. I wasn't enough for you. You wanted adventure and glory. But the words catch in my throat, like burrs.

'I couldn't stick it – being away from you. I came back. Isn't that enough?'

Another rattle. Not the window this time. The door downstairs. Seth clutches my arm tighter, his face pale, frozen, like the knight's effigy in the parish church.

'Please, Martha, help me.' His whisper is more urgent now. 'Hide me. Don't tell anyone I'm here. Please, if you ever loved me.'

And suddenly I know, but I don't want to know at the same time.

'Seth, no.'

'Please, go down. Tell them I'm not here. Please.'

Another rattle. A man's voice calling. Seth pulls me away from the window. I stagger forward, my bare feet thudding on the floorboards.

'Anyone home?'

The door downstairs has opened. I can tell from the draught that sweeps up the stairs. I want to hide, pretend there's nobody here. But suppose the stranger isn't satisfied? Suppose he comes inside, looks around for himself?

And suddenly I am stumbling down the stairs into the house, groping for each step so I don't fall in the half-dark.

A shaft of light where the door stands ajar. The sliver of a man is visible, head, shoulder, bicorn hat, a fragment of scarlet coat. The head twists in my direction.

'I beg your pardon, miss. I didn't mean to alarm you,' he says.

'Who are you? What do you want?'

My voice is as dry as straw, tickling the inside of my throat. But I know who he is. He has pushed the door wider and I can see his uniform, the epaulette on his shoulder, an officer's sash around his waist. I stay on the staircase, halfway down, where I feel safer.

He doffs his hat, tucks it under his arm.

‘My name is Hammond,’ he says. ‘I’m pursuing a deserter. Has he come this way? Have you seen anyone?’

A deserter.

I came back to you.

I couldn’t stick it.

A deserter. The shame of it, the shame. A deserter in a time of war, with Boney on the loose again…

My voice won’t come. I don’t know what to say. Only an odd little cry comes out. The officer’s gaze grows wary, as if he’s just discovered I’m a wild animal instead of the tamed creature he was expecting.

Two things happen at once. The skies open. The deluge hisses and spits and rattles against the windows, patters upon the foot-hardened earth of the yard.

And Pa’s voice calls from a distance. The officer turns, calls something back, his head still bare despite the fact he is more outside than in. The gold braid of his epaulette gleams like a rare jewel in the dark.

My ears are humming, or perhaps it’s the rain. Or maybe I’m dazed from working all day in the heat, or the unexpectedness of Seth’s appearance, or the crash of thunder. I can hear voices, but not make out words. Then Pa is ushering the stranger inside.

‘I’ll not hear of it, not in this weather,’ Pa declares. ‘Our Martha’ll fetch you a mug of ale, won’t she?’

He glances towards the fireplace, expecting me to be there, seems surprised to catch sight of me on the stairs.

Grasping for something real and ordinary, I glide down the rest of the stairs. Creep like a shadow to do my father’s bidding. The officer demurs, but somehow I know he’ll not refuse the pewter tankard when it’s set before him.

He’s telling his story again.

‘I gather he’s from this area,’ he says. ‘Seth Roberts. Perhaps you know him?’

I feel Pa send a glance at me, though I refuse to look, pretend to be busy gathering up a pile of linen I haven’t had time to iron. I must move it elsewhere, though I’m not sure where. There is but the one room downstairs, save for the larder.

‘Aye, I know him, and his family too,’ Pa replies. ‘A feckless lot if there ever was one,’ he adds, ignoring my pained protest of ‘Pa.’

The officer doesn’t say anything to this. I peep up and he’s staring into his ale, as if it could tell him the future. Or as if he’s forgotten why he’s here at all.

A boot scuffs on the doorstep. More strangers by the door.

'There's no one in the outbuildings, sir,' the sergeant says.

'Ah.' The officer frowns and bows his head.

I murmur 'scuse me' and whisk away. Maybe upstairs I can get away from all this, away from the confusion in my head, away from the officer's questions, away from Pa's pointed remarks.

I'm not even halfway up when I hear Pa murmuring to the stranger, 'Truth is, he used to come here, sniffing around after our Martha. Didn't like it above half, but what's an old man to do, without a wife to take care on his only daughter?'

I cough loudly and deliberately, making him break off. But I know coming up here was a mistake. The drumming of the rain on the roof is louder, the rooms smaller, the light dimmer. And if they should follow me…

My room seems empty. I stare around it, then jump and drop the linen on my bed when I hear a noise behind me.

Seth is behind the door, his eyes wide with desperation, his fists doubled, ready to fight his way out of the corner he has backed himself into. A wild animal, no more than that. Just as Pa always said he was.

'It's all right,' I whisper. 'I didn't say nowt.'

Some of the fight seeps out of him, like air from a pig's bladder.

'Pa's talking to them,' I add, because I owe him a spite, for leaving as he did, lured by a drum-roll and a red coat. But then I relent because I can never seem to help myself. 'Don't fret. Pa knows nowt – not about you leastways.'

'Oh, Martha,' he breathes.

His hand brushes my cheek. I know what he wants, but I slip through his grasp like water.

'I've got to go back,' I say. I can tell from the voices below that the labourers are trooping into the house. 'Knowing Pa, he'll ask them all to stay till the storm passes. And if they should hear us whispering…'

He stares at me so, it's as if he wants to eat me. I shiver. I was right; I know I was right not to let him kiss me. Kissing was always my undoing. He could talk himself out of any trouble, excuse any spell of neglect, any glance after another girl, as long as he kissed me afterwards and told me he liked me best.

I know if I let him kiss me now, I'll forgive him again and I'm not quite ready to do that yet. Not after all the whispering and pointing and giggling from the village girls, the disapproving looks and head-shaking of the older women, when they found out he'd jilted me.

'I love you, Martha.'

His words stop me at the door. For a long minute, I won't look at him.

'Aye,' I say, 'I believe you did once.'

And then I'm away again, no more clear in my mind what I should do. Because the truth is, Seth can't stay here. With the soldiers so close on his tail, what chance is there that he'll get away?

Oh, Seth knows all the hiding places hereabouts. But nobody can live like that, not for long. In a town or a city, he might be able to lose himself better, among all those other people. He should never have come back. I'm sure he would soon have found another dupe like me.

The storm shows no sign of abating. It's as dark as December in the house. There's no shortage of things to do now everyone has come in, drenched to the skin and in want of a feed. They're all a little dazed and shy in front of the strangers.

'You'll stay and sup with us?' Pa cocks his head at the officer.

'That's very kind of you, but we really ought to be going. We've a duty to fulfil.'

But Pa, being Pa, won't listen to anything he doesn't want to hear.

'There'll be enough for a few more, won't there, lass?'

I shrug.

'I'll manage,' I mutter under my breath, not wanting anyone to hear, not really, or only a bit. 'Like I always manage somehow.'

'I'll pay, of course,' the officer – Hammond – says.

Pa demurs, he insists, and I allow their words to dance above my head, amid all the other voices, as I set the table, because my mind is on another problem. There's one more mouth to feed than Pa knows of. No matter what happens, I can't let Seth go hungry. Not after all we've been to each other.

Because in my heart of hearts, I still love him, even if I no longer trust him or believe his promises.

I barely notice what is happening around me as I work. The other women have come to help, but it's a shock when I turn from the hearth and a large, masculine hand takes the heavy cooking pot from me. A scarlet sleeve brushes against my thin linen shift. Why didn't I think to make myself look more respectable?

'Thank you, sir,' I murmur, 'but there's no cause…'

He isn't listening. He swings the pot easily, lifts it onto the scarred, scored table.

'It's the least I can do to repay your hospitality,' he says, making me shrivel inside because I know I haven't welcomed him at all.

There's something in the way he looks at me that makes me even hotter than leaning over the hearth and, since there's precious little left to do, I go across the house and open the door, on pretence of seeing if it's still raining and snatching a breath of air.

It's fresh outside, fresher than it's been all day. I gulp in relief, though the rain is pelting harder than ever, turning the yard to rivulets of mud.

And then Pa is calling everyone to the table before the food is spoilt. I can see Hammond is still torn. His men are muddied and hungry. But he's also afraid his quarry might escape. And then he looks at me, as if everything depends on me.

'Thank you,' he says and signals to his men.

Pa sits at the head of the table as he always does and the officer sits opposite me. He and Pa talk of other things – the war in France and bad harvests and I hardly know what else – but I can feel Hammond watching me, though I keep my eyes fixed on my plate.

Why is he still here? Does he suspect me? Or does he feel sorry for Seth and thinks he's allowing him to escape?

My stomach is so clenched, I can scarce force myself to eat at all. Not that it'll go to waste. I'll have to find a way to convey it to Seth, that's all. If it was just Pa, it would be easy. But Hammond – how will I evade his notice if he thinks he knows my secret? Or does he intend to give me enough rope to hang myself with, and Seth too?

The labourers are growing louder now, less shy now they've had a sup of ale. It crosses my mind that if Hammond was drunk, perhaps he wouldn't see one more figure slink down the stairs in Pa's oldest coat.

But though Pa slaps him on the back and bids him drink like a man, Hammond only laughs and turns the talk another way and after those first, thirsty sips, his tankard doesn't grow any emptier.

At last he nods at the sergeant and at this signal the little band rises. My heart thuds, like the blows of an axe. The labourers too are readying themselves to dash through the rain – still steady but not as heavy as before – back to their cottages in the valley.

I go with the soldiers as far as the gate, wanting to be certain they're truly gone. But the officer lingers beside me. Though he's not touching me, I can feel him, every tall inch of him, the broad shoulders, the strong hands, the long legs.

'You know where he is, don't you, Miss Martha?'

His words are so quiet, they're barely audible above the hiss of the rain. But I flinch as if under a lash. He says it so matter-of-factly, not accusing, not demanding, not spiteful. Not anything. As if it's just an inevitable fact that he has accepted and doesn't care about much. As if it wasn't a matter of duty, or a question of life and death. I've heard what the army's like, for all I live so far away from towns and cities.

'If he gives himself up, the punishment will be minimal, might even be waived altogether,' Hammond goes on. 'We're to be sent to Brussels next week. There won't be time for much else.'

I glance at him. His eyes are hooded. Perhaps he's telling the truth and perhaps he isn't. Or maybe he doesn't know himself how it will be, because he's young too – I can see that in the better light – and things change in a time of war.

I take refuge in silence, turn my face away again to watch the rain, still bouncing off any hard surface. Surely this rain cannot last?

'It'll be the worse for him if he runs or tries to resist arrest,' Hammond goes on. 'If he comes quietly, I'll put in a good word for him.'

I swallow, but still say nothing. He shrugs.

'Just consider it,' he says and turns away.

'Wait.'

I don't know if I dare. He's gazing at me so calmly yet firmly, as if he'll know if I lie to him.

'There's a ruined hut, up on the moor.' The words seem to come by themselves. 'We used to go there sometimes. Pa doesn't know. Maybe…'

I try to meet his gaze fearlessly. It's true, every word of it. And perhaps it shows in my eyes.

'Thank you,' Hammond says, ever so gently, as if trying to spare my feelings.

I give him directions, almost as if I was in a dream. My mind is already working, trying to find a way to get Pa out of the way, so I can get Seth out of the house. Or must I wait till everyone is asleep? But what if Hammond and his men come back?

As I speak, Hammond takes my hand. He stares deep into my eyes, so I can't look away. Then his other hand caresses my cheek, tilting my head so he can kiss me on the lips.

I can't breathe. I can't move. I can't speak. Rain runs down my cheeks, drenches my hair.

Then Hammond turns on his heel, calls a command to his men and is off.

Moving as if in a dream, I retrace my steps back towards the house. I jump as Seth meets me at the door.

It's too soon. I know it's too soon.

'Seth,' I hiss, but he won't listen. He barges past, slamming me against the doorframe.

He's running now, not slinking in the shadows, but out in the open. Running in the wrong direction. And then I'm running too. I hear indistinct voices, see the pallor of a shirtfront as Hammond turns towards Seth's voice.

I see the glint of a blade in a sudden shaft of light that has penetrated the clouds. See the cluster of red-coated bodies surround Seth on all sides, grab his wrist, fight the stiff arm until the knife falls from his grasp and his shirtsleeves, gleaming white as the snow, are wrested and fastened behind his back.

'I'm sorry,' Hammond says, looking into my eyes again.

But I turn away, his traitorous kiss still burning on my lips.

The Dying Orange Bush

The orange bush in the corner of our living room
Is dying.
Its leaves are withered and dry,
Its fruit is wrinkled and bitter.

The soil is dry,
The plant is parched.
Help is reserved,
Given out only in desperate measures,
Which could take six to eight
Working weeks
To be decided.

You could be dead by then.
Six to eight weeks
The plant may starve.
Because of six to eight weeks
The orange bush in the corner of our living room
Is dying.

Dana Andersen

Spinothalamic Tract

Loving you from a distance
is like stroking a phantom limb.
I writhe for you at night,
clambering at the air
to find you gone, to find you not there.
The double negative of you
developing in the dark room of my sleep,
until shadows of red overwhelm me.

The root of the itch grows
in the graveyard of nerves
that haunts where you used to be:
in my arms, in my ears.
I swear, sometimes I can hear you
as the compulsion to itch travels the curve
of my naked, punctured spine.

It would take more to separate us than a knife,
or miles of map and road.
Still I ache, craniophagus twin,
scraping at the weeks so that
you may be re-sewn to my side.

The relief will be sweet,
like the emptying of a full bladder.
Every kiss will be dissolving stitch
so that no one can see the seam,
Then it will only be heat that rises
up my spinothalamic tract.

Until then, I scratch red in the black.

Harriet MacMillan

The Mountain

by Jonathan Page

The blue of the rock is cut with yellow streaks. Trees the colour of thyme hang in space. It is impossible to get the scale of it, the disk of the lake does not compute. The rock pulls away into the sky but it feels below him also, as if he could fall into it, through the Fauvist poles of the birches and the beeches. The red of last year's leaves slip under his deck shoes, the wrong shoes for climbing a mountain, but he cannot let this chance go. It is like grieving, being here, it is like a dream in which we die in childhood.

The path zig-zags up on a causeway of white rocks and the landscape does not change. The corners, where there is a chance to look out over the forest and the lake and the mountain opposite, fail to initiate the sublime. He is panting already, middle-age has shallowed his stamina, and he has only an hour to climb as high as he can. In theory. In theory. Perhaps he could be a little late. His new wife is waiting for him in the restaurant at the base of the waterfall. The tear in the mountain was black with damp to either side of the waterfall and made him want to fuck her, there and then, in front of all the other tourists.

He stumps on over the echoing ground, a sturdy man in a black t-shirt. The last few weeks have been the happiest he can remember in his adult life. He thinks of her on the vast bed, the slow curve of her back and hips and legs, the sheets scrambled onto the floor. The make-up and moisturisers and toothbrushes lined up over the sink in the hotel bathroom, a catalogue of a new order, an intimacy. He loves her, he loves her when he squeezes the lotion onto his palm after the fever of love making, when she is sleeping, content, on the bed, and he is aroused again, like a boy of twenty, of thirty. He loves the drum of the shower on his skin and the idea of the night, their dressing in fine clothes, the short walk into the baroque streets of the tiny ancient city. Marrying again is the best thing he has ever done.

And now he is on the mountain, and there is something like grief inside what he calls his happiness. He strokes the prickles of his new beard and dances over a minefield of sharp white pebbles, comic, a faun, a satyr even, because the sun and the sweat and the memory of his woman are sparking his lust. Walkers on ski poles come running easy down the brown slopes, past the toppled trees, ignoring the paths, finding their own paths. They are as he once was, young, or else really very old, and they have always been here, have always known the mountains which for him are a childhood memory. Brief summer holidays in the Alps with his accountant father, his little sister grumbling as they slogged, slow, up to yet another mountain hut or stream or cliff face. The flowers vibrating wires of colour in the meadows. Everything was possible then, the artist, the writer, the climber, the architect, all the dreamt of selves that never came to be. It is too late for the mountain, too late to dream now.

His wife Rebecca is reading a book of poems in a restaurant by the river. She is a poet also. He works in an office. They suit each other perfectly, the order of his days carries him clockwork into her presence at six thirty every night. She hands him wine or he cooks to the radio and she tells him about the day's tutorials and the meeting with the course organiser and the struggle for tenure. His office is too ordered to be a story, it is dull and a war, and all he wants to hear are her stories. She writes him poems sometimes, hands them to him shyly, to see if he sees the code. The miracle is that he lives with her all the time. The house he shared with other divorced office workers still feels real to him though he left it, its sweat and dirty plates, the constant sports on the tv, a year ago now. Her child is at university, she had him very young. They are alone in the flat, with a cat, and cacti that are the only plants they cannot kill, and all their books. He has never been happier.

The forest changes as the path rounds the corner of the mountain. The zig-zags are less extreme and there are fewer walkers descending. Nobody except him seems to be climbing up, perhaps because it is mid-afternoon and the climber's hut at the top of the mountain is hours away. It is cool and quiet as the path dips inwards, passes over a black stream that cuts black into the earth and which he touches religiously with his finger tips and taps onto his wrists and forehead. He looks at his watch, an expensive wedding present from her father. He should have turned back thirty minutes ago but his hunger for height, for another corner, burns in him. Her book of poems is a doorstop and the restaurant is pleasant, like a log cabin, and overlooks a river stacked with giant boulders. She will be writing a poem or absorbed in a poem or sleeping in the sun reflected from the rocks or paddling in the ice cold water. She will be all right, she understands that this walk is important to him. Another half hour and he will turn back.

He is lying, he is shameful. Failed love affairs the failed marriage the failure to write to walk to draw to be the person he thought he would be, are with him, clustered close, like the dead about Odysseus. He loves the dead, he hates the dead. They are colours, a broken feeling in the chest, and there is no hierarchy to them. Why. He is happy, isn't he? His breath is dark with the dead. He wants them, he wants to go back and make it right, but he is old now, everything is behind him. He stops to photograph a cairn made of white pebbles in the elbow of a tree branch and picks up a stone from the path to add to it and then drops the stone. Five minutes more, the path ahead is dappled with light. Light shadows swarm over white burning ground. One more view of the lake and then back and sorry I am late and forgive me my love.

The sun replaces him briefly, birds sing in the undergrowth, songs of glass echoing out of the black skirts of the wood, and he is free and as high as he has ever gone as a teenager in the Alps or nearly so. A rock leans down out of the scratch of blue sky, burning with ferns, and he touches it in prayer. Everything will be all right. He pads into the wood again, which is coniferous suddenly, a red dead floor like sleep stretching out over the shapes of small boulders. He comes to the waist-high mouth of a cave and crouches to enter it bravely. It smells of damp and there are rocks mounded up and it does not seem to go back so far though it is very black. The cave feels like achievement, his full stop. He can stop now and turn back. He takes a selfie with his phone when he's back outside on the path.

A walker appears, on poles, coming down the path to him. Middle-aged, handsome, a green water bottle in a sheath at her hip. He does not like to ask but he asks: Hello how far to the hut? And she pauses on her poles, registers his deck shoes, his arms and face cold with sweat, and says not far fifteen minutes much more time to go down again. Only fifteen minutes? About fifteen minutes, it is not far. And he thanks her and the dead thank her and his wife will be worried now but if it is so close. If the top of the mountain is just over the rise there. He walks on.

Trees hang black leafless lines over the enormous white boulders in the stream. She had to go out there to find the clear blue water, the trout hanging in their deep tanks. The surging froth also as waterfalls burst like wounds from between the carved rocks. There are circles and channels in the boulders, where the stream once ran. There are perfect circles in the rocks under the blue water, pebbles laid inside on the sand as if a human had put them there. She reached in, her arm a sudden ache of cold, to take one pebble and then let it fall again feeling the sacrilege. That was hours ago when she was sure Sam would be back within an hour and a half, as he had said he would. Her writing pad bakes with useless stubs of lines on the beach under the trees. She has no evidence but the shade feels fetid to her, unclean with algal growth. She scrapes at the white gravel with a bone of stick and finds only white gravel. She is starting to panic. Where is he? She is angry at having to worry. To be left an invalid at the bottom of the mountain. She does not even have her phone, it is on the bed, out of power, back at the hotel.

She goes back to the monster rock where she has made camp. The coat she never needed is laid out to sit on and there is the fat curling book of her hero and there is the plastic bottle she has filled and filled from the stream and all this is evidence of a far off time when she was happy to have this secret adventure of water and reading. The sun pushes her focus slant and her heel folds over as she reaches out to grip the rock which is not there. She does not fall but the sharp pebbles fall against her feet and ankles as she wades for balance. Reality lifts in sheets from the rocks, the trees, the blue sky and will not settle. She sits on her coat and feels herself flow to the pattern of the stream. She does not think of him, it is all she can do to hold onto herself. The sun. Stupid. All this time.

Last night they were drunk, happy. She wore a yellow dress in the warm rain by the river. The buildings were old, with coats of arms over the doors, and solid, like cardboard boxes set on their wings. The plaster was broken open on some houses or dusted pink. They sat at tables with their wine and looked down at the river in its elegant stone trough and did not mind the blat of the rain on their backs. They had the tables to themselves, everyone else crowded into the lit shelter of the awnings. They were special. They were not young but this man this love had found her and destroyed realism. It was good to be unrealistic to laugh at nothing again and to feel his hand on the wet skin of her shoulder. They had spent the day in their hot hotel room making love over and over until she felt too sore to go on. It was enough. It was not what she had thought she was looking for but it was enough. There was no more striving to be done. No compromises with loneliness and the ghosts of those who had gone away. Last night and today, this morning, they had been happy. Two hours ago they had been happy. In her heart, still, she was.

The fish hangs in the pale room with the ochre rocks. Sharp angled blue flowers cover the rock across the stream, under the skirt of the trees. A boy places his feet with the care of a dancer on the road of rocks to her pool and when he gets there puts his hand palm down on the deep image of the fish. The water vibrates into obscurity and there is no longer a fish. Nobody is disappointed. Rebecca is trying so hard to be herself she cannot speak and would probably not ask the boy for help if she could. He is different from her son, when he was young. This boy is spare and blonde on legs as long as a deer. He is nothing like her son. Her published book is called *The Scars*. She had meant to put in other poems, poems about light and nature and water, but the divorce was in her still, very deep, and the growing pains of her teenage boy, and those were the poems she put in the book. She had nothing for another book until she met Sam. Now she can write about water. Now she can.

With difficulty she drags the great book of the poet she admires and unconsciously imitates at times in under her arm. She makes a tent of her body over the coat and then hauls that up too. She almost drops the book. The bottle of water is more important but she has no more hands. She drops the coat and tries again, picks up the bottle this time, and then, with the tips of her fingers, hauls the coat up onto the flank of the rock. Are you okay? A tall thin man is on the beach, he looks like the boy, he is a father and English also. She wants to keep him away with a joke but she finds it hard to speak. She thinks she has a spot of sunstroke. She needs to get out of the sun. The man picks up the coat and the book when she drops them and she clutches at his arm like she is drowning. Help me.

She wakes in a room with wooden walls. She sees a green awning through the window, round green tables and chairs and their hire car under the spindley trunks of the pines. The light is grey and the cars that were parked next to their car have gone. At first she feels only peace and cannot remember how she got here. There is a blanket over her sun pink legs and her book is on a chair by the single bed. The hanger of shadow under the awning seems to extend into the room and limit the world to this. There is no age to her. Then there is the fear, it is overwhelming, perfect. The disaster is already present to her though in theory it is still the future and another outcome is possible. There are coats hanging on hooks by the door, they must belong to the staff but she cannot explain the bed. Maybe the manager stays over sometimes or a security guard. Maybe this is a home as well as a restaurant.

Help me please it is my husband he should be back by now. The mountain. He is up there. I do not have a phone, my phone is at our hotel. The chairs are on the tables and the till is covered with a soft beige hood, like a sleeping hawk. The woman who was wiping the counter slowly wipes her hands with a towel. Do you understand English? Yes. I get manager, okay? I get manager. The woman does not see the emergency, maybe it is her invention, part of the sunstroke. Sam is probably in the car, on the phone, also out of his mind with worry, wondering where she has got to. She thinks this and knows there is nobody in the car. She can see the car through the square window in the restaurant door. She looks at her watch. Seven thirty. Sam left her by the river five hours ago.

It is an hour not fifteen minutes climb to the mountain hut. The sky grows dark with rain and where the path crosses bare rock he sees channels scarred into it, from ancient streams. Flowers grow in profusion in lush vaginal segments between flat patches of rock. He is still surrounded by trees, but they are short and twisted like orchard trees, and he can see the high peaks jagged and grey under the blackening sky. His thighs hurt, he is his breath, he is light with the disease of guilt, he is coming to the brink of something he will not name. He steps over a hole in the ground gridded with rusted iron and wonders if this is a dugout from the first war, a store for ammunition perhaps, or just a hole. He takes a picture to show Rebecca and instantly deletes it. He walks in a small anteroom, shut in by the sky, a small circumscribed space, where the path curls tighter and the incline grows steadily less. The lake is a spot of dark blue at the base of an immense vertical forest and the mountains, the true mountains, do not fit the frame of his camera phone.

The hut is not a hut but a vast wood-clad dormitory when he finds it. He pushes open the wooden gate and steps into its garden. There are two tall young men in the garden, clad in yellow anoraks, with helmets tied to their slim backpacks. They look at him like an alien or an animal and he is conscious of the fact that he is wearing a t-shirt and baggy tourist shorts and deck shoes fit only for paddling across a car park. He feels the urge to die more strongly now, it is okay to call it what it is, now that his hands are on the slatted fence set over the void. He tries not to look at the men checking through their equipment, he tries to look like he knows what he is doing.

The mountains are as bare as a planet and the sky rolls black through their sharp teeth. There is a plain below them bleak as Mordor and that is where the young men, older, wiser than him, more familiar with wonders, are heading. One of them looks at a map in a plastic cover and then they walk away, heading for the big wooden sign that points to the next hut, the proper mountain hut, another four hours walk away. He wants to be them. He wants to go out to the vast grey falls of shale and find snow on the backs of the boulders. Already his nostrils are sore with altitude. What would it take to die out there, where he has always dreamed of being?

The woman follows Elizabeth out of the restaurant into the hanger of green shadow under the awning. Tables and chairs block her way and prevent her ignoring the calls of madame madame. The woman has an old Nokia in her hand and mimes phoning. Call the police, you call. A metal chair vibrates, alive, under her hands as she drags at it, for support or to symbolically continue her escape out into the light. The ground glows white, boundless beyond the line of the awning. Her head aches and she feels she might vomit. Thank you that is kind, and speaking, she feels she might fall to her knees. The air is electrified as with all endings.

She walks towards the car, the phone in her fist. Birdsong falls out of the trees up river and she sees the ripple of silver between the rocks where it waterfalls. The cliff face is pink with dying sun and the gorge blackening already with night. The woman walks behind her, her hands a little outstretched in anticipation of her falling down. Phone police? You phone husband? The black block of the phone a weight she does not know what to do with, it feels too much of an effort to start pushing numbers. Then, impossibly, the passenger door of the car is wide open. Did she open the door? Has it always been open?

Hello Rebecca I am sorry. I am sorry. Sam is sitting over the squash of his belly, his arms pale, dangling, on the edge of the passenger seat. His cheeks are apple red and he is shivering. The rage begins a black howl somewhere far back in her. Contempt. Hate. The whole house of sorrow that is life. All that shows is her tap tap tap of the old phone against the roof of the car. He gets out of the car and tries to put his arm about her shoulder but she shrugs, hating his touch, more than she has hated anything before. How could you, she whispers, unable to speak for the woman who stands behind them, watching them. I am sorry he says very flat, his whole being shallow and without energy. Sorry. You are sorry. Yes I am. You are sorry, is that all you can say?

But this is not the end, despite her anger and the anger it triggers in him. He has been to the house of the dead and she is black with what he has done. But still, still. There is the spell of happiness still on them. Rebecca beats at his chest with the black phone until it bruises.

~ The End ~

Cover Art by Mark Sheeky

Mark Sheeky is a professional artist based in Crewe, Cheshire. The epitome of the multidisciplinary creative, Mark is an oil painter of detailed imaginative paintings, a music composer and publisher, a performance pianist, author, radio broadcaster, and computer programmer. He exhibits and performs widely, and has one painting as part of the permanent Cheshire art collection. His writing style is as surreal and inventive as his artwork, and his first novella, The Many Beautiful Worlds of Death, was published in 2015.

Cover artwork: *The Outcast*

Previous anthology artwork:
The Ball of the Future

You can find out more about Mark's varied work on his website,

www.marksheeky.com

More Prizewinning Fiction from *Earlyworks Press*

We at Earlyworks Press invite the winner and a selection of the shortlist from each of our writing competitions to submit work for an anthology. We are proud of the standard, variety and entertainment value of the resulting collections. Here is a selection…

Short Stories

Stories, long and short ***The Ball of the Future***
ISBN 978-1-910841-25-9 **£8.99**

The Several Deaths of Finbar's Father
ISBN 978-1-906451-96-7 **£8.99**

Don't look down! ***Ways of Falling***
ISBN 978-1-906451-30-1, **£8.99**

So many things only get noticed when they aren't there. ***Significant Spaces***
ISBN 978-1-906451-86-8 **£8.99**

Flash Fiction & Poetry

Flying colours, flowing colours, falling walls and courting pigeons: ***sharp as lemons***
ISBN 978-1-906451-95-0 **£7.99**

Kitchen magic, holiday islands and football in a flower: ***Writing on Water***
ISBN 978-1-906451-37-0, **£6.99**

There is generally £100 or more prize money for first place in the competitions, always a free copy of the anthology and discounts on other books for authors (email services@earlyworkspress.co.uk for details), as well as the option of a discounted membership of the Earlyworks Press Writers' Club.

If you would like to see your work featured in an Earlyworks Press anthology or would like more information about our publishing and book events and activities, or to order books, please visit the website:

www.earlyworkspress.co.uk